The Caring Teacher

How to make a positive
difference in the classroom

Rob Potts

First published 2021

by John Catt Educational Ltd,
15 Riduna Park, Station Road,
Melton, Woodbridge IP12 1QT

Tel: +44 (0) 1394 389850
Fax: +44 (0) 1394 386893
Email: enquiries@johncatt.com
Website: www.johncatt.com

Opinions expressed in this publication
are those of the contributors and are not
necessarily those of the publishers or the
editors. We cannot accept responsibility
for any errors or omissions.

ISBN: 978 1 913622 90 9

Set and designed by
John Catt Educational Limited

Reviews

A wonderfully warm, encouraging and realistic overview of teaching with practical tips for topics ranging from safeguarding and building relationships to report writing and teacher self-care. Rob has created a close companion, not only for Early Career Teachers but for veterans wanting to reignite that spark and remember why they got into teaching in the first place. Thank you for sharing your knowledge and experience with us!

Sophie Smith-Tong, founder of Mindfulness for learning.

————

The Caring Teacher is an inspirational handbook, packed with practical guidance to help teachers in all stages of their career to perform their roles and responsibilities with young people's interests at heart. Rob's guiding principles of care and integrity shine through and remind us that we can all make a difference to our students.

David Alcock, teacher, founder of Hopeful Education,
and educational blogger and presenter.

————

Rob Potts has created an engaging and down-to-earth insight into the lessons he has learned in his teaching career. *The Caring Teacher* contains often rib-tickling reflections on the reality of creating a positive learning relationship.

Although this is by no means a how-to manual, Potts' writing manages to balance a guiding hand with practical notes on everything from lining up to parents' evenings. *The Caring Teacher* supports the reader in their pursuit of becoming exactly that, by encouraging them to develop their own personality and strategies within the classroom. It is a worthy and enjoyable read, with a giggle or two along the way.

Chris Dyson, headteacher at Parklands Primary School
and National Leader of Education.

———

Paths into teaching are always interesting to read and Rob's path, which he uses so well to illustrate this incredibly useful book, particularly so. Rob draws upon his own experience to give prospective or new teachers a wealth of tips and advice. Reading it would inspire more experienced teachers too. An EBD school is a fine place to start your career and Rob's experience here allows him to really dig down into what behaviour management means and how you can manage the most difficult of classes.

I loved the moral base from which Rob writes. Having a child of his own with SEND informs lots of his advice – which is so ridiculously useful and sensible! He is right that 'gobby' is not a million miles from 'articulate' and there is a way into working with every child. Every child really does matter and building relationships is key to your success. 'Nobody goes into teaching for an easy life,' Rob says, but this book will certainly help you to find your way into a very rewarding career.

Paul Garvey, education consultant, author and former
Ofsted Lead Inspector.

———

An education world where the 'I' is present for everyone is the key focus of *The Caring Teacher*. Powerful questions, looking at our words differently and positive ways for self-awareness are the key themes. A great book to support our new normal where caring and being kind is the new currency to help everyone. Thank you Rob for such an inspiring book, a book for change, a book that will guide everyone whatever stage they are at in their career.

Tracy Shand, CEO Exeat Together and author.

———

I loved this book. So often, in the teaching profession, we start out wanting to make a difference to the young people and families we work with, but lose sight of this in the maze of professional standards, data, progression demands and paperwork. Rob reminds us all the way through his book of the ways in which we show care and nurture in the profession while also meeting all the demands on our time. He presents balanced perspectives on a wide range of professional experiences and seeks to offer guidance and insights into sustaining integrity, particularly for those teachers in their early careers. I'd highly recommend this book for all teachers entering the profession: it's a great read, friendly, relatable, and full of practical advice and tips as well as addressing the bigger questions around sustaining a caring professional identity.

Amanda Nuttall, Senior Lecturer for Primary Education
at Leeds Trinity University.

'Love many, trust few, always paddle your own canoe.'
Katie (Reprographics), Eckington School.

To Joan, for always being there and for instilling the right values from day one. And to Sheila – the most committed, compassionate and fierce colleague one could wish for.

Thanks also to all my frazzled colleagues for hanging on in there, the parents who have been such valued allies over the years and to the most important people (the kids) for providing daily reminders of why we keep putting ourselves through all of this!

Contents

Foreword

Gosh, Rob – why didn't you write this 56 years ago?

When you first asked me to pre-read this book, *The Caring Teacher*, I was immediately struck by the fact that the focus and content were so similar to our recent publication, *It Takes Five Years to Become a Teacher*. I worried that the books would be too similar and for the first few pages my worries seemed to be justified. And then you started...

So many great tips, so many amusing anecdotes and some dos and don'ts that would have really helped me in those first five years at Normanton Secondary Modern. One section that especially struck home was the section on language in chapter 5. It was 1965 when I started teaching and nobody ever talked to us – as trainee teachers – about the need for positivity, encouragement and language. I had hated school myself – and I had hated teachers. As a breed they seemed uniformly negative, aggressive and to share a common dislike for me. How I ended up being a teacher has always been somewhat a mystery to me. College was an early escape from sixth form, but at that time I had no intention of entering the profession when I left.

My early learning of how to teach all took place 'at the coal face' in Normanton Secondary Modern, in a West Yorkshire pit town. The teachers there, the only role models I had, also seemed to spend their days snarling and sneering at the students, who – in turn – ignored them for the most part. With a book like this, I would have found better routes into communication with those disaffected and demotivated pupils.

I love the way the book advocates finding a positive way to address two serious issues in one: the eternal struggle and lack of self-belief alongside the pupil's perseverance. And the advice on pupils' wellbeing would have really been an asset when I returned to England after many years abroad and restarted my career at Great Horton Middle School in Bradford. I loved those five years in an inner-city middle school, with its interesting mix of highly motivated and disaffected students. I made so many mistakes, particularly with the thirteen-year-olds who were in my Year 8 classes for two years. I encouraged them to share their worries and concerns in private diaries that only I read (and never marked) and then found I had promised never to disclose the horrors that some were experiencing in their lives. Rob's book would have guided me through the process of supporting those adolescents so much more effectively.

Yet one of the most moving sections for me was reading the great advice on watching out for the lonely child on the playground. I *was* that child – not just lonely but abused many days of the week, yet no member of staff ever stepped in with a kind word of encouragement or support, and not one adult intervened on my behalf.

I attempted to make myself invisible for the last two years of my primary school education, avoiding the other children and lurking furtively on the fringes of the playground. Yet some days they would refuse to let me fade into obscurity and came seeking me out with shouts of abuse and name calling that still make me cringe today. And if – in heading towards the school doors at the end of playtime – I inadvertently came too close, they would run screaming as though from a historical leper, fending me off in mock horror. And the two statutory teachers on yard duty each day would turn a blind eye and ignore my humiliation. Would that the teachers in my primary years had read that chapter and watched for the lonely, scared child!

Thank you so much Rob – reading this essential guide for those entering the profession or seeking further support just flew by!

Ros Wilson
Cert.Ed. Dip.Ed. M.Ed.
Education Consultant 07866 581623
Ros@BIGWRITING
@RosBigWriting

Introduction

When I first entered the teaching profession we were bombarded with all sorts of technical guidelines and advice: marking policies, how to plan a three-part lesson, assessment for learning, the difference between aims, objectives and outcomes. All bases were covered – often in infinite detail. Once I stepped into a classroom, however, I quickly realised that unless you can forge effective relationships with the students and quickly get them *on side*, much of this know-how can soon become redundant.

As I progressed through my career, I noted a tendency for people to assume that relationship building and pastoral care were natural gifts that you were either good at or you weren't. I also encountered teachers who would openly acknowledge that 'this isn't really my strong point' or 'I don't do pastoral.' As one of those teachers with a supposedly natural aptitude for this side of the job, this attitude always irked me somewhat and I wondered whether it would be as acceptable for those of us drawn to the pastoral element of the role to say, 'Teaching and learning isn't really my thing.' I suspect not.

The fact is that to be an effective teacher you need to be able to master both the academic and pastoral side of your role proficiently; the success of one usually predicates the other. Moreover, empathy, emotional intelligence and, where required, diplomacy are all skills (not natural gifts) and, like any skill, they can be developed with hard work and a willingness to grow and develop yourself.

I wrote this book with the aim of helping others to unlock these skills within themselves. Whether you're just embarking on your teaching journey as a trainee or ECT or if you're a more experienced professional looking for fresh approaches to benefit your practice, there is advice here that I hope will make your classroom a happy and productive workplace for you and your students. I've also shared some of my own experiences as a teacher – including one or two where I've got things badly wrong – and hope that this can inspire, reassure and possibly even amuse you.

The important thing to take from this book is this: you may have been drawn to the teaching profession for all sorts of reasons but, if you wish to be successful, care needs to be at the core of everything that you do. Teaching can at times be an incredibly taxing – and occasionally soul destroying – vocation but, if you focus on putting wellbeing and happiness at the front of your agenda, you'll quickly find that it can be the most rewarding and enjoyable job in the world.

CHAPTER 1:
Starting out

So you want to be a teacher? Great! It's a brilliant job, the career prospects can still be pretty good and, if you're prepared to put up with the bumps in the road and remember why you started out down this track in the first place, it can provide you with moments of sunshine on a more regular basis than pretty much any other job I can think of. But, before you click *send* on that email and sign your life away to the Department for Education, there are a few things that you need to know.

First things first, it's not going to be the way things are presented on those expensive adverts they use to hook young, idealistic dreamers onto a journey of fulfilment and transformation on prime-time TV. The advertisers present an alluring image: attractive young go-getters, with glowing complexions and sharp business dress; rows of smiling students, transfixed by their idealistic young teacher; moments of inspiration amidst strategically placed Bunsen burners and an uplifting soundtrack. All good.

What they don't show are the bags under the teachers' eyes, gathered after spending all night planning a lesson, or those many moments of despair and doubt wondering, 'Why do they behave for their regular teacher but not for me?'

What they also fail to mention is the reason why they have to spend so much money on costly recruiting campaigns and generous financial incentives for trainee teachers anyway: as an Early Career Teacher (ECT), there's still around a 33% chance that you won't make it beyond your first five years in the classroom. These figures are improving but that's still an attrition rate that's comparable to the Battle of the Somme.

Surviving the first year

Even if you're one of the hardy souls who makes it back to the trenches unscathed, there will be a need to accept that, if you're going to make it to the pot of gold at the end of the rainbow (your Teacher's Pension!), you're going to have to find a way to make this work – and keep it working – until you're 68! No amount of energy, idealism and (that increasingly dreaded word) *resilience* is going to keep you upright and functional for the next four decades – no matter how good the holidays are.

So unless you're prepared to grind doggedly through your prime adult years or join the reported one-in-three teachers who plan to quit the profession altogether within the next five years, you're going to have to establish a sustainable approach to teaching.

Actually, scrap that. Life is far too short for us to simply get by and 'make things work'. You need to find a way to make the job fun and rewarding and keep it that way. And hopefully that's where this book can help.

No amount of energy, idealism and resilience is going to keep you upright and functional for the next four decades – no matter how good the holidays are.

Before I leap straight in and reveal the secret formula for finding the fun, I should probably start by telling you a little bit about myself and my own route into teaching. I'll start with the first plot twist: unlike a lot of those who gravitate towards a career in education (often without a pit-stop in between) I hated school. *Really* hated it.

As a 'reasonably bright' working-class kid from Salford, I eschewed the opportunity of a scholarship at one of the region's better independent schools (smart move 11-year-old me!) and instead followed my mates to a low performing and, frankly, rough local comprehensive school. What followed was five years of fights, bullying, copying down from OHPs (ask your parents!) and a complete lack of fulfilment. Whenever I sit marking books, being sure to provide encouragement, reassurance and clear, constructive comments, I'm always left scratching my head and wondering whether I ever received such helpful feedback from my teachers. And the answer is, I don't think I ever did. However, as I was (as I may have mentioned) reasonably bright, I managed to pass my GCSEs (unlike a frighteningly high proportion of my peer group) and was able to move on to A-levels at the local sixth form college and eventually a degree. From there, as someone who as well as being reasonably bright could also write a bit, I moved on to a career as a sports journalist. So far so good.

Now, at this point, the prospect of ever returning to school, let alone as a teacher, would have been absurd. School had been a time in my life to be endured, rather than enjoyed, and my abiding memory of teachers (aside from a few honourable exceptions) were of middle-aged men with tweed jackets and stale breath who would occasionally emerge from a smoke-filled staffroom to bellow at you or instruct you to stand staring at a wall until the dinner bell had sounded. This was not a life path that I would have envisioned for myself.

When I talk about my past life in the *ever-so-glamorous* world of sports journalism, the response from many people (not least fellow teachers) is incredulity: why would you give up that lifestyle to be a teacher?

It's true, being a sports journalist can be incredibly exciting and enjoyable and it's certainly a pathway I'm still happy to encourage my students to head down if they harbour the ambition. During the years I spent in journalism, I covered major events, encountered a few famous people and met many great friends. I also (unknowingly at the time) developed a range of skills that have served me well in my current career. As a sub-editor, I sharpened up the grammar and proofreading skills that have come as second nature to me as an English teacher; I became perilously accustomed to working to tight deadlines; and when you've delivered a live match update for the radio on a freezing afternoon at The Shay, in Halifax, the prospect of a Key Stage Three assembly holds little fear for you.

Looking back, it's tempting to wonder, *why the hell did I give that up?* But at the risk of sounding trite and worthy, the one key thing I lacked was fulfilment. Although working in the press box at a Grand Final sounds exciting, much of the day-to-day work of a sports journalist revolves around reporting on the banal minutiae of sport and satisfying the appetite for rolling 'news' – you can literally spend a full week reporting on the state of someone's hamstring!

The other thing that I lacked as a sports journalist was that indescribable buzz you can experience when something you've done can completely transform someone's day – or even their life.

Being able to make such a positive impact on the lives of others on a day-to-day basis provides you with a sense of satisfaction that few experiences can match.

There's a reason why hairdressers are consistently ranked as the happiest workers in Britain: having someone plant themselves in your chair feeling like a dog's dinner and then watching them strut out feeling like a million dollars must provide a sense of job satisfaction few other careers can come close to matching. Being able to make such a positive impact on the lives of others on a day-to-day basis provides you with a sense of satisfaction that few experiences can match.

And so it was I decided to ignore the well-meaning advice that flowed from friends and family – including my mum, who had worked as a learning mentor for over 20 years – and made a change in career that I've rarely regretted.

Once I'd made this decision – with my dreaded 30s edging perilously into view – my route into teaching was also fairly unconventional but provided me with a holistic insight that has been invaluable, both as a classroom teacher and, later, as a senior leader.

I decided pretty early that I didn't want to be one of those people who started teacher training and either dropped out mid-course or made it into my NQT year and then decided it wasn't really for me. I also harboured memories of my own unfulfilling school days and wondered whether a return to a school environment was really going to be right for me. So I decided that, before I even thought about which teacher training route I should opt for, I ought to gain some *shop-floor* experience working in a school and, when the opportunity came up to work as a teaching assistant at a school for kids with Emotional and Behavioural Difficulties, I jumped at it.

For those who have never worked at an EBD school, let alone one that was firmly in the crosshairs of Ofsted, I can tell you that it was an experience that could probably warrant a book of its own. But it was also an experience that provided a bedrock for my own career that has proven to be absolutely priceless. If you can cope with being sworn at, accidentally kicked in the privates (yep, that happened!) and spending a healthy chunk of your working day coaxing kids off the roof, you can cope with anything. More formatively, however, as a teaching assistant you could almost feel *invisible* at times, like a scullery maid tiptoeing silently into the parlour of a country house with afternoon tea, and this gave me an incredible insight into the behaviour of teachers and not only how they treated me as a lowly teaching assistant but also how they presented themselves and how they managed relationships with other members of the school community. It's an experience that continues to instruct me in my own teaching career – particularly in my role as a leader – and one that I'll draw upon throughout this book.

As a teaching assistant you could almost feel invisible at times, like a scullery maid tiptoeing silently into the parlour of a country house with afternoon tea.

My year as a teaching assistant (which included working with the progeny of some of the more high-profile members of the city's criminal fraternity) was invaluable and it's an experience that I would recommend to anyone who wants to enter a career in education with a more rounded skill set and more realistic expectations. It was now time to start thinking about the most appropriate route into teacher training though.

The big choice for me was whether to opt for a more traditional Postgraduate Certificate of Education (PGCE) or go for the 'learn on the job' approach, which at that time meant finding a school wishing to host me and a university willing to accredit me on the Graduate Teacher Programme (GTP).

Nowadays, there is a whole range of 'on the job' options and many schools favour schemes such as *Teach First* and *School Direct* as they enable them to cast young recruits in precisely the mould that their organisations desire. This route was particularly enticing for me as, having already worked in education for a year and with a mortgage to pay, the prospect of earning a full-time wage while I trained was really appealing. Ultimately, however, I backflipped and went for a PGCE and, for me at least, the ability to call upon the support of other trainees in my subject specialism and to have the time to step away from my training schools in order to reflect on what I had learned, proved to be extremely beneficial. I still often hear younger teachers arguing about the relative merits of both of these pathways and those who have adhered to schemes like *Teach First* tend to be particularly loyal (and even messianic) when discussing the merits of their chosen route. The truth is that there are pros and cons to both pathways and the decision for anyone embarking on this journey is to figure out which one best suits them.

You're a teacher, Harry!

Whichever training route you decide upon, after a year as a trainee, you'll be ready to embark on the next stage of your journey: navigating your way through your ECT years. During your year of Initial Teacher Training (ITT), you will have hopefully had the opportunity to observe some outstanding practice by experienced colleagues, and you may well have witnessed other lessons that will have appalled you and, fuelled by the arrogance of youth, you may even have thought to yourself, 'If I ever teach a lesson that bad, you can shoot me.' As someone who may have occasionally shared those very feelings, I would strongly urge you to hold that last thought until you have spent a few years in the classroom and understand that occasionally circumstance will dictate that the only thing you need to focus on is somehow making it through the next 50-60 minutes. The one thing your ITT year will undoubtedly see you laden with, however, is a heap of misconceptions, and in this section I'll attempt to identify some of the biggest whoppers for you to look out for and hopefully reject.

Respect is earned

Perhaps the most common and most career limiting misconception that hobbles ECTs is the assumption that becoming a teacher will automatically confer you with a level of respect and, once bestowed with that metaphorical sheriff's badge, those around you will automatically bend to your will and follow your commands unquestioningly. *It doesn't and it won't.*

Becoming a teacher won't immediately bestow you with respect. You have to earn it. And it will take time.

Just like in any other walk of life, respect is something that you will have to earn. And it will take time. If you were once a high-achieving student who was motivated and well-behaved (as many future teachers probably were), it's easy to see where this misconception took root. You probably enjoyed school life, respected the status of your teachers and were desperate to seek their approval. For a lot of children though, at least two thirds of this mentality does not apply. For many kids – at the time at least – school is not a place where they enjoy being; often it is somewhere that imposes a structure upon them that they are not keen to embrace and presents them with a set of hopeless challenges that they don't feel able to meet. For many of those same children, teachers aren't role models and they aren't authority figures who must be obeyed; they are alien figures from a world that is different to theirs, whose sole purpose is to impose that restrictive regime and force them through a series of impossible and demoralising tasks. With that in mind, it is hardly surprising that many children do not believe that their teachers' respect is something that they desire or need. Yet ultimately – as I will try to outline later – the teacher's ability to establish mutually respectful relationships and confer appreciation for any positive achievements they can seize upon, are perhaps the two biggest factors in bringing the best out of young people.

There is still a lot of groundwork that needs to go in before you are able to reach that point so, in the meantime, I will leave you with the following simple (yet essential) maxim: *respect has to be earned and it has to be shared.*

'Pupils won't misbehave if it's a good lesson'

In the teaching world, there's a maxim that you will inevitably have rammed down your throat verbatim from the start of teacher training and then, periodically, at inset days and training events throughout the duration of your career. The premise is simple, it appears to have a fair amount of logic attached to it but it is also absolute nonsense. However, I guarantee you that it won't be too long before someone tells you: 'Pupils won't misbehave if it's a good lesson.'

I'm not sure who came up with this particular whopper but it's one that is still pervasive, is utterly wrong and is often used to inflict shame and guilt upon teachers when things go awry in the classroom. It would be tempting to attribute a falsehood of this nature to Michael Gove, during his short yet impactful time at the DfE, but this dogma goes back well before his time and has been parroted endlessly for as long as I can remember. But I can tell you one thing: it's not an expression that was either coined by a child or indeed anybody who has any understanding of children and adolescents.

I'm not sure who came up with this particular whopper but it's utterly wrong and is often used to inflict guilt upon teachers when things go awry in the classroom.

For the avoidance of doubt, there is no disputing the fact that, if your lessons are well planned and engaging, you are likely to find behaviour management much easier. However, despite the best efforts of those who ought to know better to propagate this myth, it is far from a simple cause and effect scenario.

This is probably one of those areas where those teachers who have made the transition from being poachers to gamekeepers are at a slight advantage. If you were once one of the 'naughty ones' during your own school days you will know already that no lesson ever conceived can be as interesting or engaging as the story your pal on the next desk wants to share with you. And, even if your teacher, Professor Hawking, is about to reveal the origins of the entire universe on his interactive whiteboard, you are likely to be more fascinated by the lewd symbol that one of your classmates has daubed on the wall behind his desk.

Effective planning is one of the key weapons in your armoury but there are lots of equally essential skills that you will need to develop in order to crack behaviour management.

The truth is that the quality of your lessons is one of the most important factors in effective behaviour management but it is far from the only factor. You could spend every second of spare time outside of the classroom planning meticulously and producing the most beautiful resources but that will not guarantee that 9B is going to behave during period five on a Friday afternoon. Similarly, the teacher next door may be teaching to the exact same lesson plan as you (or perhaps even an inferior one) but their class may be fully engaged and behaving impeccably. The fact is that there are far more variables in play than the content of the lesson plan – and some of the most critical factors don't always come naturally and take time to master.

Effective planning is one of the key weapons in your armoury but there are lots of equally essential skills that you will need to develop in order to crack behaviour management. In the meantime, ignore the member of staff at the front of the hall at inset (they probably don't really believe what they're saying themselves). Cut yourself some slack; you're going to have good lessons and you're going to have bad lessons. Sometimes you're going to be on top form and, on other occasions, you are going to have a stinker. Don't blame yourself, learn from each of those experiences and invest the time in developing the full array of skills that will make you an effective classroom manager.

Kids are rarely the problem

If ever you hear someone try to steer you away from a school because 'the kids there are terrible', your inclination should always be to walk away from that person and disregard any advice they proffer you in future – certainly where teaching is concerned. Kids are rarely – if ever – the problem.

You can work in challenging schools in deprived areas where the students' values and motivations are not guaranteed to immediately gel with the educated, middle-class values that you have cultivated – even if you come pre-loaded with your own working-class credentials (trust me, that card holds limited value!). Your job as a teacher is to find the commonality that enables you to bring the best out of those kids, not to mould them in your own image.

Similarly, if you're assuming that finding your way into a *leafy lane* suburban state school or – better still – a cosy little private school is the key to an easy life, think again. The kids might get dropped off in nicer cars but this environment presents its own set of challenges.

Whether you are dealing with kids who are hobbled by physical, emotional and intellectual deprivation, low aspiration and distrust of authority, or those who are entitled, demotivated and may even look down their noses at the teachers, with their inexpensive hatchbacks and comfy shoes, the students at whichever school you work at are going to present their own unique challenges. That's the job you signed up for.

It takes a special individual to look at the group in front of them, analyse their strengths and weakness and then seek to bring the absolute best out of each individual.

One of the most depressing comments I have ever heard was from a colleague who told me that he was looking to move onto another school in order to 'work with *more academic* students'. As an unapologetic idealist, this comment floored me. To borrow a footballing analogy, it has always been my view that, as teachers, we should always aim to be more like Jürgen Klopp than José Mourinho. Virtually anyone can take a group of hand-picked high achievers, sprinkle a little fairy dust, watch them shine and then bask in the reflected glory. But it takes a special individual to look at the group in front of them, analyse their strengths and weakness and then seek to bring the absolute most out of each individual. That's teaching!

You will find some groups and individuals are harder nuts to crack than others and you will almost certainly find that, even in the longed-for 'good school', this will often vary from class to class and year group to year group. Fixing these idiosyncratic puzzles and finding the perfect alchemy within each class can be one of the most challenging – but also one of the most rewarding – elements of the job. It's what we do and developing this particular skill set is at least as important as sharpening your subject knowledge. As one of my former headteachers once astutely remarked to a colleague of mine: 'You're not a teacher of maths; you're a teacher of children.'

The truth is it's not the behaviour or academic prowess of the students that is likely to render somewhere either a rewarding place to work or a hell hole; it's the calibre of the management.

I'm assuming that anybody reading this will be doing so in the hope that they won't join the growing ranks of those who decide that teaching is no longer for them. So I'll furnish you all with some simple but essential advice, whether you're looking for your first job or your next job: do your homework!

Ofsted reports are the usual go-to for teachers on the lookout for a potential new school but they only paint a limited picture of what a school is really like to work in. My advice is to dig deeper. Reach out to friends (and friends of friends if necessary) to find out what the school is *really* like. Ignore superficial features such as facilities and even location and get to the nitty gritty. What is the Senior Leadership Team like? Is it a happy, inclusive staffroom? Is there a high staff turnover?

Also, even if you reach the interview phase, never lose sight of the fact that this is a two-way selection process: you are choosing whether the school is right for you, every bit as much as they are choosing whether you are right for them. Treat the interview process in the same way you would view a house you are thinking of buying. Grab any opportunity to talk to those already at the school, outside of the confines of the process if possible; look beyond the carefully choreographed timetable for the day and keep an eye trained for potential cracks in the ceiling. Always follow your gut; the person interviewing you (most likely your potential future boss) is likely to be on their best behaviour but, if you're getting negative vibes, don't be afraid to politely and graciously withdraw from the process. If you fall into the wrong post, it can quickly transform teaching from a dream vocation into the job from hell, where every passing weekend is punctuated by the 'Sunday night fear' and you find yourself living for the holidays and dreading the start of each new term. Treat choosing a new school with the same care that you would finding a new partner: only commit if it feels absolutely right!

Most importantly, don't allow your natural competitiveness to propel you into the wrong job. Yes, you may well want to *win* the interview process and prove yourself the best candidate but remember: there is an abundance of teaching roles out there and your only priority has to be landing the right one.

Kids rarely are the problem in a school;
poor leadership sometimes is. Choose carefully.

There are plenty of supposedly challenging schools out there where the relationships you build, the camaraderie in the staffroom and the presence of a caring and supportive leadership team will make going to work each day a pleasure (and banish that Sunday night fear!). Equally, there are 'high-performing' schools, often draped in shiny new buildings, where the atmosphere is oppressive and each working day (while you are able to endure it) will be a nightmare. If you're genuinely passionate about pastoral care, be sure to find a working environment where the staff are afforded the same level of nurture, care and respect as the children.Kids rarely are the problem in a school; poor leadership sometimes is. Choose carefully.

Respect your elders

In the world of boxing the term *journeyman* is used to describe those fighters whose ambition has long expired but who can still eke out a living by turning up each weekend and doing enough to avoid serious harm but not enough to ever win. The term journeyman is generally used in a disparaging way but actually the word has far more noble origins. The word's roots are derived from the medieval trade guilds and it was used to describe skilled workers who had successfully served their apprenticeships and were now effective practitioners of their trade. Unfortunately, the more modern interpretation of the word has won over and anyone labelled a journeyman is assumed to be an undistinguished professional loser whose only interest is in cashing the next pay cheque.

That cranky old teacher shuffling around the staffroom could be you one day.

Sadly, in teaching, a similar myth has been allowed to develop and older, more experienced staff are often unfairly categorised as being ineffective and marking time until their retirement. One or two schools are particularly keen to propagate this narrative when indoctrinating young, enthusiastic trainees and it can sometimes be expedient (for all sorts of reasons) to squeeze out older, more expensive staff and fetch in young, cheap and more malleable replacements.

As an inexperienced teacher, however, you'd be well advised to reject this myth and *pay some respect to your elders*. Maureen in the English department might be a little cantankerous but you can guarantee that her subject knowledge is encyclopaedic and she's probably forgotten more about actual pedagogy than you know. By the same token, Alan in geography may be riddled with gout and might even be prone to the odd faux pas but he's gathered 40 years of working knowledge of the dark arts of classroom management and has the kind of unshakeable ethics that we should all admire. Neither of them can probably parrot any of the in-vogue educational buzzwords and they'll each have witnessed countless fads rise, fall and then rise again in a monotonous cycle. In any other working environment though, you'd be soaking up that kind of accumulated knowledge like a sponge, so it's tragic that in our trade there has been a conscious drive to write off our most experienced practitioners as 'past it' and (often) usher them on an undignified journey towards the knacker's yard.

For the sake of your own development, you should avoid being part of that cattle drive. More importantly, if you last the course, that cranky old teacher shuffling around the staffroom could be you one day.

Learn your trade first

The other narrative that seems to have gathered pace over the past decade or so is the *cult of premature ambition*.

I'll talk about this particular phenomenon and the pitfalls associated with it during the final chapter but, in the meantime, I'll leave you with a simple warning: don't be rushed into trying to run before you've really learned how to walk.

Another common (and infuriating) trope that I've witnessed many times over the years is that of really capable and committed teachers being disparaged for 'lacking ambition'.

Devoting yourself to being an outstanding teacher is a noble ambition.

I worked with an outstanding languages teacher called Lesley very early in my career and I can remember her being tarnished with the 'lacking ambition' barb. Her response was immediate and should be instructive to anyone who is serious about having a worthwhile career in education: 'I am ambitious; my ambition is to be an outstanding teacher.'

As far as I know, Lesley is still working at the same school, is still the same kind and committed professional who I was able to lean on for support as an NQT and is still delivering outstanding lessons to classes full of happy students. That's outstanding teaching and there should be no more noble ambition than that.

Unfortunately, for reasons we'll explore later, too many ECTs are bloated (and often exploited) with premature ambition and promises that 'If you follow this path, you'll be on SLT within three years.' It's tempting rhetoric but ultimately, if you want to achieve credibility and longevity, it's worth thinking carefully before being reeled in. My advice would always be: learn your trade, earn respect, enjoy what you're doing and, once you've earned the rewards and are fully equipped to be a good leader, go for it!

Never be told by someone else that you're not good enough

Inevitably, if you stick around long enough, you are going to come into contact with some good bosses and some bad bosses. That's life unfortunately.

There's also every chance that you may come across people who will seek to diminish you and undermine your confidence for all sorts of reasons. Just as in life, you have to make a decision about whose opinion you value and can trust and whose you need to learn to ignore and disregard.

Teaching is tough and it also brings with it huge, potentially life changing responsibility. If you're not quite cut out for it, there's no shame in walking away. In fact, given the responsibility that you hold, it can be a noble decision and one that can lead you towards a path that you're more suited to. But don't be ushered down that path by anyone other than those you trust the most and those who have your best interests at heart.

I've seen too many talented teachers squeezed out of the profession by people who – for all sorts of reasons – have taken a dislike to them. Don't be one of the victims of this cull. Nobody will know better than yourself whether this is the life for you but – if in any doubt – only seek the guidance of those who really care.

The world according to Derek

Hopefully that has helped dispel a few pervasive myths and you're ready to get into the nitty gritty of classroom management and outstanding pastoral care. Before we get to that though, I want to end this chapter by introducing you to Derek.

During my PGCE, the course was led by Tim, a genial bear of a man who'd enjoyed a distinguished career in education and was now happily imparting his years of experience on the next generation of aspiring teachers. Tim was a beloved figure among our cohort but his occasional sidekick, Derek, was a slightly more divisive character. Derek was a little older than Tim, was also a retired teacher and was at an age where even his time as a lecturer was creeping towards its final act. Derek was unapologetically *old school* and was prone to the kind of off-colour remarks that would leave some of the cohort bristling and others quietly sniggering, but it was clear that, although he harkened from a bygone age, he knew his stuff.

When the day finally came when he was ready to hang up his boots as a lecturer too, he rather theatrically sauntered away after leaving behind four golden rules which have stuck with me throughout my teaching career and which I'll share with you verbatim below.

1. There's always a negative corner in the staffroom; avoid it like the plague. If you get sucked into that corner, the negativity will be

infectious and it'll blind you towards all the many joyous things that being a teacher can bring.

2. Never try to be *too good*. Work hard, do your best for the kids but always know when it's time to down tools and accept that what you've done is good enough. If you don't learn this lesson, you'll burn out quickly.

3. When you're a form tutor, you're likely to come across a troublesome lad in your form – a real handful. Don't write him off. Get to know him; find out what he likes to do. If he's a footballer, make sure you're there to watch the school team the next time they play – no matter how busy you may be. Next time you see him, tell him how well he played. He'll know from that that you care and, once you've built that relationship, he'll be on your side forever.

4. Gentlemen, before you set foot into any classroom, always check your flies!

And then, with those brief words of wisdom still wafting in the air, Derek left.

CHAPTER 2:

Guiding principles

This is a short chapter but, along with the final chapter, it's probably the most important one (at least if your reasons for entering this profession stretch beyond enjoying the holidays, climbing the greasy career ladder and then looking forward to a superannuated pension).

There's some dispute (at least in our house) over whether Alexander Hamilton or Chuck D is responsible for the maxim 'If you stand for nothing, you'll fall for anything' but, as a teacher, these are words that you ought to consider from time to time.

As I've stated previously, there is no ambition more noble than committing yourself to being as outstanding a teacher as you can possibly be. If you're a maths teacher – aside from fulfilling your safeguarding obligations – there's no problem if your number one priority is to make sure your students are as capable a group of mathematicians as they can possibly be. And, if you're a PE teacher, it's perfectly acceptable if your main goal is for all of the students in your class to enjoy physical activity and learn to be competitive, controlled and resilient in the process. But if you've got the opportunity to be so much more than a classroom teacher, why not use it?

Some of the children in your care may not come from households where their parents are either capable or interested in being effective mentors. Some of your students will have grown up in communities where there is a paucity of positive role models and where the path of aspiration barely stretches beyond the outskirts of the estate. And some of your students may be so desperate for guidance that they might look to YouTubers or reality TV stars for inspiration. You have chosen a vocation that provides you with the opportunity to fill that void and, as another great man once said, 'With great power comes great responsibility.'

I really hope that, as teachers, we're all not only equal to that challenge but willing to embrace it. But in order to do so we're first going to have to wrestle with some pretty big questions of our own.

If you're going to preach a particular doctrine, you need to be prepared to live it too. Kids can spot a fake a mile off.

Firstly, what sort of school are you willing to buy into? As the first chapter makes clear, choosing the right school will be a huge factor in determining whether your career is going to be rewarding or a wrench. For instance, if you're not religious, how comfortable will you feel working in one of the increasing number of faith-based schools? Even if you don't share that particular faith, can you find enough commonality in the values and ethos to enable you to be a genuine advocate of the school?

Working in a school is not like working in a bank. You're choosing a set of values that you're going to have to buy into yourself.

Similarly, are you going to be at your most effective working in the high-pressure environment of a selective grammar school? Would you be happier in an environment where nurture and care are the top priorities? Or might it be possible to find a happy medium?

Working in a school is not like working in a bank or a supermarket. You're choosing an institution with an identity and a set of values that you're going to have to not only buy into but also advocate sincerely yourself. You have to choose carefully and you have to be 100% comfortable with that choice – otherwise you're in the wrong place.

You then have to decide what kind of young people you want to be responsible for developing. Much of this will, of course, be dependent on those values already determined by the school, with most schools these days having ditched the old Latin mottos and replaced them with an array of 'core values'. Nevertheless, within your own classroom, there's still plenty of scope for you to determine how you present and prioritise those values and what your basic expectations for those around you are.

You'll also need a code or a set of professional standards that you hold yourself accountable to. For me, these particular standards pretty much wrote themselves when I became a dad for the first time halfway through my NQT year. Later, as we learned that my lad had Special Educational Needs and we found ourselves being routinely let down by the education system, these strictures were fine-tuned and solidified. Regardless of whatever expectations Ofsted, the Independent Schools Inspectorate (ISI), or whichever school I happen to be working at may impose, my own professional code is simple and unshakeable: if what I do wouldn't be good enough for my own kids, it isn't good enough for the kids I'm teaching. There may be occasions where I have to be kind (and realistic) with myself and accept that occasionally circumstances are going dictate that my best is going to have to be *good enough*, but that's a line in the sand I drew for myself a long time ago and it's a line I still work hard every day to maintain. If and when I ever find that I'm unable or lack the motivation to reach that line, I'll know it's time to stop and find something else to do with my life. In the meantime, it's this self-imposed threshold that keeps me focused and keeps me honest.

Finally – and most critically – you need to decide what kind of teacher you want to be. What are your own values? How do you seek to present yourself? What kind of relationships do you seek to establish? This *identity* has to be true to you. I've seen many teachers who – for whatever reason – try to create classroom personas and, more often than not, they're embarrassing and tend to have the opposite effect of whatever they may have been intended to achieve (e.g. faux 'strict' teacher tends to actually come across as odd/deranged teacher). You have to think carefully about how you present yourself and the values you wish to impart but it has to be genuine – it has to be you.

And here's the most important part: if you're going to preach a particular doctrine, you need to be prepared to live it too. Kids can spot a fake a mile off.

CHAPTER 3:
Setting out your stall

When you enter the teaching profession or even move to a new school, one of the first tasks facing you is to establish your presence, both physically and metaphorically. First impressions really are everything in our profession; if you come across as a soft touch, kids will quickly sense weakness, look to exploit it and any attempt to toughen up will often be shrugged off and seen as a bit disingenuous or – worse – sad. Conversely, opting for *strict* and attempting to wave the metaphorical sheriff's badge we talked about earlier – particularly if that's not a persona that's true to you – may well put you across as cold, unapproachable and unpleasant. I have seen this approach work for some people who (behind the mask) are actually lovely, funny and affable but it's not a facade that I could maintain – nor would I want to.

It all comes back to the issue we looked at in the previous chapter: *what kind of teacher do you want to be?* There are certain attributes that I would argue are non-negotiable: firmness, fairness, commitment, consistency, patience, empathy, passion for the subject, a lifelong love of learning and – above all else – kindness. But, as I've hopefully already made clear, the most powerful and sustainable 'persona' you can adopt is your own. That's not to suggest you adopt a 'take me as you find me' approach, over-share personal information or, worse still, fall into the trap of being the kids' 'pal'. Your professionalism and the cast-iron boundaries that brings with it should be tacitly understood by everyone – but you still need to be *you*. The students will respect that, you'll enjoy your time in school much more and, what's more, you'll already be acting as a positive role model and imparting an essential life lesson without even realising it!

We'll come back to values and relationships in due course, because they're at the core of everything we do. But before you go into your first lesson, there are a few less abstract issues that you will have to tackle.

Establishing a positive learning environment

If 'an Englishman's home is his castle', the same is even more true of a teacher and their classroom. Whether the environs of your school are state-of-the-art, opulent or downright crusty, it's essential that you establish and sustain a learning environment (and a set of associated routines and expectations) that allows you and the students to perform at your absolute best.

The battle to defend that castle begins before you even open the drawbridge and I'd suggest a set of clear routines that precede and signal the end of every single lesson.

1. **Insist that the students line up outside your classroom (on time and quietly) at the start of every lesson.** This essentially allows you to dictate the *narrative* of the lesson before you even set foot in the classroom. The students are aware that there's a physical boundary that has to be respected and – critically – you're the one who's in charge of that boundary. If you're fortunate and your colleagues on the corridor apply the same expectation and are supportive/collaborative, it also protects you from those 'grrrr!' moments that will occasionally cause even the saints among us to be a minute or two late (jammed photocopiers; fights on the playground; unavoidable toilet breaks; I could go on!). The important thing is that this simple routine allows you to wait until the students are settled and ready to learn before you even permit them to cross the threshold of your classroom. The alternative is that you walk into a classroom where the students have already entered and, as a consequence, you may end up spending the first 5-10 minutes of the lesson trying to settle the class. Control the narrative.
2. **Try to have a settler activity on the students' desks to engage them as soon as they enter the room.** OK, honesty time here: this is one of those *ideal world* suggestions that, when you're already working flat out, you may struggle to find time to achieve. What I will say from

personal experience is, when I do find the time to do this, it is an absolute game changer. The content of this settler activity can vary from subject to subject but, whether it's a photocopied wordsearch featuring key terminology, a cloze exercise or (the English teachers' favourite go-to) a spot of silent reading, it's well worth building this habit into each lesson in order to settle the students into the classroom.

3. **Use the register as part of your settling in period but also as an aid to reflective learning.** While it might be tempting to silently complete the register while the students are completing their settler task, the register itself can be a great way to engage the students, signal to them that there'll be no *passengers* during today's lesson and reflect on prior learning. This can be as basic as telling the students that, when their name is read out, they need to respond with a designated key term or recall something that they learned during the previous lesson. However, it's a simple routine that requires minimal planning on your part and provides plenty of worthwhile benefits in terms of both behaviour and learning.

4. **Always impose a seating plan.** This may seem like *Teaching 101*, but having a predetermined seating plan is so important, even though the most experienced among us may occasionally lapse and allow the students to sit where they want. I could probably devote a chapter to the merits of a carefully considered seating plan but, in the interest of brevity, I'll keep this relatively succinct. First up, however calm and considered your classroom persona and regardless of the mutually respectful relationship you've established with your students, this is a reminder that, ultimately, this is your classroom and you're in charge. Once you've established this control, the make-up of your seating plan is equally important and needs to be carefully considered. The simple part of this is situating those individuals who are likely to distract one another as far away from each other as possible. However, there is a range of other elements that you'll need to factor into your plans. For instance, if you know that Sean sees every lesson as a potential stand-up comedy gig, the last place you want to stick him is at the back of the classroom where his every utterance is likely to trigger 30 swivelling heads. Likewise, if you know that Saira is bright but lacks confidence, your skill as a manager of people is to pair her with

someone who is likely to empower her to show what she is really capable of. There are also SEND and medical factors to take into consideration. Which students need to be close to the teacher's desk? How can the seating plan be maximised for the benefit of your teaching assistant(s)? Do any of the students need to be within easy access of the exit? Whether you have a narcoleptic child in the room who needs to be safely pinioned between a classmate and the wall or you simply wish to keep Ebony and Maya as far apart as possible, an effective seating plan is essential.

5. **Enjoy the silence.** If you have followed these first four steps, everything is working like a charm and the students are engaged and beavering away in perfect silence, don't let anyone or anything disturb it – least of all you. We can sometimes convince ourselves that, if we are silent for too long, we are somehow redundant; this couldn't be more wrong. This is teaching, not radio broadcasting. There is no such thing as 'dead air'. The moment we utter something as benign as 'Is everybody doing OK?' or 'Does anyone need any help?' we're inadvertently puncturing an atmosphere of near-silent productivity that many teachers would kill for. Try to savour those moments of calm engagement. It probably means you're doing your job well and frees you up to float around the classroom checking on progress and issuing the odd strategic thumbs up and smile. If you do spot one of your students heading down the wrong path, either delay your intervention until a less disruptive juncture can be found or try to issue support as quietly and realistically possible. When you hit upon these moments, you have ventured into teaching utopia; enjoy it!

6. **End the lesson on your terms.** 'The bell is for me, not for you' is a battle cry that probably resonates from many of our own school days, as well as a cliché that we've all cringingly uttered ourselves since entering the teaching profession, but it's a statement that is rooted in necessity if you're intent on sustaining an effective learning environment. Your ability to maintain this precept is predicated on the effectiveness of your planning and timing – something that even some of the most able and experienced practitioners never, ever quite master. One of the golden rules I maintain in my lessons is that, if a student asks a relevant question about the topic we're covering, we'll always

endeavour to explore it; as an educator, it seems counterintuitive to stifle inquisitiveness. The obvious downside of this is that, once you venture down these rabbit holes, the five-minute discussion that you'd factored into your lesson plan can suddenly morph into something that takes much, much longer (but may be nonetheless rewarding) and your meticulously crafted lesson plan has suddenly gone out of the window. The fact that you've had to adapt your plans suggests that you're doing something right; stimulating and then satisfying curiosity is at the heart of good teaching. What matters, however, is that you don't allow this welcome digression to detract from your all-important routines. You need to reinforce courtesy and good habits, even when you are on the back foot. The students shouldn't be packing up (let alone shuffling in their seats or standing up) until you tell them to; they do need to focus fully on the plenary and not the impending break bell; they should know that they won't be allowed to leave until they're standing silently (and sensibly) behind their desks with their shirts tucked in. And, yes, it's a cliché but the bell really is for you, not for them!

Getting the classroom layout right

Once you've established positive habits, your focus needs to shift to the make-up of the room itself – your classroom layout is far more than just feng shui! There are a number of creative ways in which you can configure your classroom and plenty of sound pedagogical arguments for and against each of them. In time, you can experiment with each of them and see which of them work best for you but – at least at the start of your teaching journey – I'd always advocate focusing on the basics.

Whenever I see inexperienced teachers set out their classrooms in a horseshoe configuration, I'm often struck by the image of the Boer lieutenant Adendorff in the movie *Zulu* as he draws the shape of the 'buffalo horn' formation in the Natal dirt and warns Stanley Baker and a young Michael Caine of the manner in which the Zulu general Cetewayo plans to encircle and then wipe out their overstretched and overmatched defensive lines. You may not be facing a 2000-strong enemy force but I always worry that, as an ECT or indeed as an experienced teacher seeking to establish yourself in a new school, the horseshoe configuration can potentially leave you exposed to the risk of being overwhelmed in a similar manner.

Whenever I see inexperienced teachers set out their classrooms in a horseshoe configuration, I often worry that this layout can potentially leave them exposed to the risk of being overwhelmed.

Arranging desks into clusters is also fraught with risk at this stage, when you are still battling to establish yourself and impose your expectations. The problem with clusters is that, with the students now facing each other, you're potentially turning one class that you're trying to manage into a series of smaller classes. In this scenario, your attempts at behaviour management can quickly start to resemble the infuriating seaside arcade game *Whack-A-Mole* – as quickly as you get one cluster settled and on task, the group behind your back have started talking or have lost focus.

There are some really sound educational benefits to laying your classrooms out in this format but, while you're starting out, I'd always advocate the KISS approach (keep it simple, stupid!) and lay your classroom out in rows, with your students seated in strategically chosen pairs.

Just positioning yourself silently beside a student's desk will sometimes be enough to encourage them to get on with their work.

This configuration does have its limitations (particularly when it comes to group work) but it also has a range of benefits for any teacher entering a new environment. Firstly, it removes a number of the variables you'd otherwise have to consider when instigating a seating plan and all eyes are automatically on the front of the classroom (i.e. on you!). Secondly, it makes it much easier for you to weave your way around the classroom with as little fuss as possible, supporting students where necessary, monitoring their work (or lack thereof) from behind their backs and positioning yourself strategically when required (sometimes just positioning yourself silently beside a student's desk will be enough to encourage them to ignore any previous distractions and get on with their work).

Once you've established yourself and your expectations and have developed some of the other skills detailed elsewhere in this book, feel free to get creative but, in the meantime, keep things simple – and effective.

Applying the behaviour policy

Here's a statement that may ruffle a few feathers but it's rooted in truth: most behaviour policies are (at their core) pretty generic. Whichever type of school you're working in, each policy will have a set of rules; some of these diktats will be clearly defined and some will be more nebulous and open to interpretation. Similarly, some schools will be fairly liberal on certain issues while others will be more hard-line. Whichever way the wind happens to be blowing, they are rules and, once you take a job at the school, it's your responsibility to enforce them (if you're not comfortable with those rules, you're at the wrong school).

Here's a statement that may ruffle a few feathers but it's rooted in truth: behaviour policies are pretty generic.

Schools will also have a prescribed continuum of rewards and sanctions, often displayed in an easy-on-the-eye graphic/table (pyramids are popular but other shapes are available!) on the school website and classroom walls. Again, different schools will skew the balance in terms of *the carrot and the stick* and some will favour slightly more draconian sanctions but, in the grand scheme of things, they are variations on a well-worn theme. Nevertheless, they are cast in stone and your job is to apply them as effectively (and consistently) as possible.

All schools must have a behaviour policy and all teachers must follow them (with a healthy dose of common sense hopefully applied) but it's worth remembering that they are there to act as a framework – they do not equip you with a *magic bullet*. Whatever your policy looks like, ultimately you will live or die by the respect you earn and the quality of your relationships.

Whatever the policy, it's the application of it and the manner in which you convey your message that really matter. It's essential that children understand the link between their choices and the outcomes they experience but it's equally important that we, as teachers, navigate the delicate line between understanding context and using our judgement while still remaining consistent. The best analogy I can offer when looking at behaviour policies is to compare them to national security: you need a strong and visible line of defence in order to project the image of security; ultimately though, it's the quiet diplomacy that happens behind the scenes every single day that actually keeps the peace.

It's not uncommon to come across teachers who struggle with classroom management (and often relationships in general) and have a tendency to fixate on policy ('In my last school, if a child misbehaved, you could ring a bell and a member of SLT would immediately arrive on a zip-line, taser the child and then they'd spend the next week cryogenically frozen in an abandoned warehouse'). Please don't be one of *those* teachers!

Policies are important and need to be reviewed regularly (with meaningful input from frontline staff) but it's the way that you implement them that's important. With that in mind, here are a few handy hints that might help:

1. **Know the policy inside out.** Your class is likely to include a number of highly qualified *barrack-room lawyers*, waiting eagerly to pounce upon any failure to follow policy on your part – particularly if it relates to their behaviour! Make sure you know the policy inside out (particularly the sections on classroom management). To help with that, it's always worth having a printed copy of the policy in the top drawer of your desk and to review it periodically.

2. **Apply the policy consistently (but sensibly).** This may seem like a statement of the obvious but those same barrack-room lawyers will be equally eager to pounce upon any perceived example of injustice or – heaven forbid – favouritism. Don't give them the opportunity. Sometimes, your professional judgement will tell you that a discreet word or a quizzical raised eyebrow (I once had a colleague who could deliver an inset on how to implement this particularly niche skill) will be enough to have the desired effect but, generally speaking, aim to stick diligently to the policy that's set out.

3. **Use the vocabulary of the policy explicitly and clearly.** This may feel a little forced initially but, if your classroom behaviour continuum features a set of step-staged warnings, use them. This not only signals to the whole class that you are implementing the policy to the letter but also removes any scope for ambiguity later. It may seem like semantics but saying, 'Right Britney, that's the last time I'm going to tell you...' is a world away from, 'OK Britney, that's your final Formal Warning and if you do it again...'

4. **Remove the emotion from the situation.** This is another case of invoking *Teaching 101* but, if you ever allow your emotions to take over your handling of a situation (at least outwardly), you've already lost control. As a teacher, you should never be upset by a student but you can (and often will) be upset by their choices. This is another reason why using the vocabulary of the policy (and the language of choice) is such valuable practice.

5. **Always favour the carrot over the stick.** Although we may wish it to be the case, we can never assume that *doing the right thing* is the default position for most children and we should never take good choices for granted. One of the most common mistakes that even the most experienced teachers make is that they instinctively reach for the stick (often neglecting the carrot altogether) and then wonder why after a while it doesn't work particularly well. There's a reason why all good behaviour policies focus primarily on rewards, with sanctions held in abeyance when those rewards don't do the trick. It's a cliché in educational circles but one of your key jobs as a teacher really is to 'catch them being good'. If that sounds a little bit wishy-washy, ask yourself this: when do you work at your best? When your manager

sees your value and regularly acknowledges your good performance? Or when your boss is constantly on your back or only notices you when things go wrong? Ponder that and then remind yourself that kids are basically mini adults.

6. **Use your carrots carefully.** We've already established that there should be no moratorium on praise; good choices should be recognised and rewarded as often and as enthusiastically as possible. We also need to be mindful that absolute consistency is an impossibility and our application of rewards and sanctions needs to be tailored to meet the likely responses of the individual. However, we need to remember that the ultimate purpose of rewards and praise is to reinforce good choices and to promote the merits of these behaviours to others. If Claire has made a career out of terrorising the school, you should leap on any green shoots of reformation, shower her with praise and reward her accordingly. But you should always be wary of crossing the line between encouragement and bribery. If you do stray beyond that boundary, you could quickly find that your recognition of Claire's demand for extrinsic rewards has sent a silent signal to the rest of the class that poor behaviour can pay off. Reward your Claires and your Connors when you 'catch them being good' but always do it fairly and in a manner that doesn't cheapen Tariq and Tiana's consistent good choices. Moreover, if you become too reliant on material rewards, it can become unsustainable and can cheapen the message you should be trying to embed: I want you to do the right thing because it's the right thing and I'll always praise you when you do. Remember, praise and encouragement can both be delivered for free, will have a much more meaningful impact and, more importantly, can always be tailored to the precise needs of each individual.

7. **Never be afraid to admit when you've got something wrong.** Occasionally, on those occasions when Friday afternoon with 9B really is frighteningly reminiscent of the Battle of Rorke's Drift, your emotions are going to get the better of you and you are going to make mistakes. That's fine; we're all human. One of the most emotive triggers for children is the feeling of unfairness or injustice. When you do make a wrong call, you'll become only too aware of this very quickly. It's important that you don't get caught up in this moment and allow

yourself to be challenged publicly; if you do, things can descend into a feeding frenzy very quickly. It's equally important, however, that if you have potentially got something wrong, you quickly find a discreet and appropriate time (either during the lesson or at the end) to talk things through and put things right. If you don't, you'll find that those trusting, mutually respectful relationships that you've worked so hard to build can evaporate pretty quickly.

CHAPTER 4:
Building relationships; earning respect

If you don't get round to reading another chapter of this book, this is the one that really nails down the *big ideas* that underpin the entire philosophy behind both behaviour management and pastoral care. Whatever the context of your school setting, however effective and supportive your Senior Leadership Team is and whether the group of students sitting in front of you are angels or demons, you will live or die by the strength of the relationships you build.

You may have outstanding subject knowledge and your understanding of pedagogy may be second to none but, in terms of the benefit to your students and your own enjoyment of the job, strong, professional relationships are at the core of what we do. And there's no more important relationship than that between the teacher and their students.

Now, before we discuss relationship building in more detail, there's one thing we need to make really clear: the students are not and cannot be your friends. While the aim should be to establish honest, trusting and cordial relationships with each of your students, if one of them ever utters the phrase 'Mr X is more like a mate than a teacher' you should know that you've inadvertently strayed over the wrong side of an uncrossable professional boundary. This can be a particularly difficult line to negotiate for younger teachers who, in some cases, may be little more than 3-4 years older than some of their students, but it's a line that needs to be firmly established and maintained. You can be friendly, you should be supportive, but you cannot be a *friend*.

Once you've established that boundary and – as discussed earlier in the book – have figured out who you are and what kind of teacher you want to be, you're then free to build the kind of strong relationships that will bring the best out of your students and make teaching a job that can be filled with regular moments of joy and satisfaction.

Find something to like – about everyone!

If the strength of your relationships with students is the thing that can make or break your career, this first piece of advice is the key to it all: find something to like about every single student you teach!

To some of you this may sound simplistic and trite and to others this might even sound impossible but it really is at the heart of all successful student–teacher relationships. People like to be liked and kids are far more likely to behave and work hard for someone who likes them and is on their side. Your job is to find that bit of something that makes every child you teach unique and magical.

In many cases this will be really easy; kids are brilliant and if – as I would hope – you've been drawn to the profession because you are passionate about working with young people, finding that drop of magic that sets each of them apart from their classmates should come easily. The trick with the 'good kids' is to then try to alert them to ways in which that positive personality trait can be an asset in life. Children's kindness, humour and determination are all attributes that will serve them well in life and it's essential that you make each child aware of the power of those gifts – particularly if they are the type of child for whom traditional academia can be a challenge. As we shall discuss later, your interactions with your students can be powerful (and should therefore be carefully crafted) and this kind of positive affirmation is one of the first essential steps.

Children's kindness, humour and determination are all attributes that will serve them well in life and it's essential that you make each child aware of the power of those gifts.

For some children, of course, finding that magic can be more than a little challenging. Often, the children who keep their light buried the deepest are the ones who actually have the lowest regard for themselves, and therefore it's even more essential that you dig deep and find it for them. Whether it's the negative affirmation imposed by their home environment, the feeling of being a square peg in a round hole or plain old poor self-esteem, these children will often work hard to prevent you from finding the positives (and often leave you wondering whether there are any!). But for many of these kids, you might well be the last adult with the skills and the determination to find that glimmer of something special that could alter the course of their lives so, please, keep digging.

Your job is to find that uncut gem of a personality trait and provide the coaching necessary to turn it into a positive.

One thing you can sometimes do is take something that could usually be viewed as a negative and subvert it into being something altogether more positive. Belligerence is a close cousin to determination; ill temper can be an unrefined derivative of passion; and, with a little polish, 'gobby' and articulate don't have to be a million miles apart. Your job is to find that uncut gem of a personality trait and provide the coaching necessary to turn it into a positive.

The one thing that will unite most of your students is that, if you like them (and show it), they will like being in your lesson and will want to please you. That alone leaves you well placed to bring the best out of your students.

Be prepared for the worst

This might sound counterintuitive in a profession where having 'high expectations' is such a pervasive mantra but be prepared for those expectations sometimes not being met. That doesn't mean that they aren't important or that you shouldn't express your disappointment when students fail to reach the lofty standards you've set for them but it's an acknowledgement of something that you should never lose sight of: you've chosen to work with children.

Your stock refrain of 'I'm really disappointed' should always be followed by the restorative question 'How are we going to put things right?'

Just like adults, children will occasionally get things wrong but they'll tend to do it more often and (occasionally) more spectacularly. Be prepared for those stumbles and, while the controlled response of 'I'm really disappointed!' can be helpful, try not to over-egg it. The most effective relationships are always built on honesty and trust, and your aim should be to foster relationships where the students are comfortable enough to be honest about their mistakes and trust you to help them to fix them. Your stock refrain of 'I'm really disappointed' should always be followed by the restorative question 'How are we going to put things right?'

If you're really not equipped or willing to tolerate the fact that kids will sometimes get things wrong or fall short of expectations, you could always head off in search of that mythical school where all the 'good students' reside. You might be looking for a while though.

For the rest of us, it's important to keep our standards but avoid allowing these expectations to become a millstone around our own and the children's necks.

Establish honesty as a core principle

Once you've accepted the fact that kids – like the rest of us – can sometimes get things wrong, the next thing is to figure out how to start putting things right. That should always start with honesty.

I have a particular maxim that I use repeatedly in these situations: *I can forgive most things but I can't forgive lying*. Once you've established honesty as the principle that sits above all else and – equally importantly – you have earned your students' trust, you make it far easier for them to start being accountable and owning their choices, and you can begin to look at how to put things right.

Always give the students a way back

This next step is predicated on honesty but actually the two stages enjoy a symbiotic relationship. With the acceptance that kids will make mistakes and the understanding that honesty is the best policy, there comes a need to ensure that once they have 'fessed up' you give the students the chance of redemption.

This doesn't necessarily have to take the form of a 'get out of jail free card' or even a reduced sentence but it does come with the tacit understanding that the willingness to own up mitigates whichever crime precedes it. This bargain is not one that will present itself immediately because it relies on mutual respect and trust between teacher and student but once those parameters have been established, they'll save both parties a lot of time and heartbreak.

If you shout loud, they'll shout louder

Being able to manage your own expectations (or at least your response to those expectations not being met) is a key skill for a teacher. You will sometimes feel disappointed, you may even feel frustration, but the only emotion you should ever allow to roam off the leash freely is care. The moment anger rears its head, however, you're in trouble and have already effectively lost control.

When it comes to behaviour management, the one thing that unites the overwhelming majority of the most effective practitioners is that you will rarely hear them shout. When you do occasionally detect a raising of decibels, the chances are that it is a controlled pantomime designed specifically to invoke a prescribed response and you can usually assume that the students are sitting open-mouthed and in silence while thinking the same thing: 'This must be really serious because Mrs X *never* shouts!'

When it comes to behaviour management, the one thing that unites the overwhelming majority of effective practitioners is that you will rarely hear them shout.

Conversely, if you happen to teach next to a classroom where the walls regularly reverberate with the roar of an angry teacher, you can also make a number of assumptions. Firstly, Mr Y has little control of either his emotions or his classes; secondly, his bellowing has long since become white noise to the students and has little – if any – impact on their behaviour; thirdly, the students probably don't enjoy being in Mr Y's lesson; and finally, neither does Mr Y!

The other problem with being a shouty teacher is that you're effectively starting an arms race: you shout first, they'll shout louder! There really isn't a winner in this battle and it certainly doesn't constitute a sustainable method of classroom management.

Even if a student initiates the shouting, that doesn't present a green flag for you to fire back. Your job is to model appropriate behaviour, not to show that you're more powerful (or at least louder) than they are. Sometimes, the most appropriate answer to shouting is silence, followed eventually by a considered response ('I'll talk to you once you can address your point more appropriately').

Even if a student initiates the shouting, that doesn't present a green flag for you to fire back.

A teacher's voice is a powerful tool and an incredibly versatile instrument, capable of great nuance if utilised correctly. A firm and clear 'bass' can bring a room to silence within seconds, particularly if used in tandem with your body language, hand gestures and facial expression. Conversely, a softer, calmer tone can evoke both empathy and a calm authority, while also subliminally signalling that those around you need to lower their decibels too. Why use such a sophisticated instrument for shouting and caterwauling when all you're actually doing is modelling an inappropriate response, raising your own stress levels unnecessarily and signalling to those around you that you've lost control?

The former Great Britain rugby league coach turned TV analyst Brian Noble once uttered a memorable line that could have been conceived with teachers in mind: 'You don't have to be a madman to be the bad man.' In other words, although it's sometimes helpful (and perhaps necessary) to be assertive and formidable, never allow yourself to lose control.

Pick your battles...and your battlegrounds

Another trap that teachers fall into is not only allowing their emotions to dictate their response, but also viewing any challenge to their authority as a gauntlet that – once thrown to the ground – they are duty bound to pick up. Rather than defending your authority this call to arms can actually erode it further (and more publicly!) and result in you being drawn into a battle where only one of you is bound by the rules of chivalry.

During my days as a teaching assistant, I can remember a Year 10 student called Leo who was big, brash and ever so obnoxious (I'll admit, finding the *magic* here was a challenge!). On one particular occasion, Leo decided that the bell signalling the end of lunchtime didn't apply to him so, as the other students sauntered inside, he perched himself on top of a large plastic rubbish bin and refused to budge. What could have been – at worst – a minor delay escalated as, despite the coaxing and cajoling of numerous members of staff, Leo refused to budge. As he began to sense that he was suddenly the centre of attention, Leo began to pound his fists rhythmically on the bin, while issuing the repetitive refrain 'Deal with it! Deal with it! Deal with it…'

Now what should have been patently obvious here was that what Leo really craved was an audience. However, being inexperienced and fearful of having my 'authority' challenged, I picked up the gauntlet and provided Leo with the attention he was after. Big mistake.

Eventually, after half an hour or so of me trying to be good cop, bad cop and everything in between, Leo's voice was hoarse, his fists were numb and he was starting to get a little bored by the whole performance. Sensing this falling action, an older, more experienced and streetwise teaching assistant walked over casually and asked Leo, 'Are you coming in now?' And, with that, he hopped off the bin and trotted nonchalantly to his lesson. After a few moments of disbelief, I gathered my thoughts and followed suit, having learned an important lesson.

That may well have been an extreme (and slightly surreal) example of what I am talking about here and spending a year in an EBD school may well have equipped me with a tolerance of just about anything, but I've been able to apply what I learned that day on an almost daily basis during the 16 or so years that have followed it. You really do need to pick your battles – and your battlegrounds.

You need to choose the behaviours that you're willing to tolerate and follow the behaviour policy of the school consistently but you also need to use your judgement to decide when to pick up that challenge. When Harrison walks into your lesson five minutes late and interrupts your introduction, does it serve you to disrupt things further by asking him why he's late or would your point be better made at the lesson's conclusion (at which point he may assume he has got away with his tardiness)? Similarly, as passionate as you may (and should) be about maintaining the school uniform policy, do you gain anything by pulling Amy up for her new pink highlights just as you've got the class settled for an end of unit assessment or would it be more expedient to save this battle for later?

You need to choose the behaviours that you're willing to tolerate but you also need to use your judgement to decide when to pick up that challenge.

Even when a student brings the challenge to you, avoid being dragged into a confrontation that you can't necessarily control, deny the student the audience they may well be seeking and choose to tackle the issue at the time that works best for you.

Accept that the students will sometimes do things wrong but try to direct them to the *right things to do wrong*!

A big part of your job as a teacher is to somehow convince your students – even the most difficult ones – to do things they don't actually want to do. You may believe that a history lesson at 8.45am is the perfect start to the day but there will be at least a handful of kids in front of you for whom bed, Xbox or breakfast would be far preferable. For the most gifted among us, the quality of our teaching may be enough to blot out the memory of those competing attractions and for others sheer force of will may win the day, but some of us have to rely upon our understanding of what makes kids tick and occasional Jedi mind tricks.

It occurred to me very early in my teaching career (around the time I discovered that my DfE sheriff's badge wasn't working, in fact) that, as much as we try to instil positive behaviours, certain kids quite enjoy doing the *wrong thing*. It then dawned on me that for these particular individuals it might actually be expedient to convince them that the thing that I actually wanted them to do was somehow mischievous or rebellious.

The best (but perhaps most extreme) example of this occurred while attempting to teach poetry to a group of archetypal 'difficult Year 11 boys'.

After being met with blank faces and the occasional grunt I spontaneously decided to tell the eight disengaged lads sitting in front of me, 'We should really be doing this outside underneath that big tree but Mr Rogers (the head of department) will kick off if he catches us.'

Instantly, Ashley, the group's alpha male, responded, 'Don't worry, sir, he won't catch us' and, before I knew it, the nine of us were commando crawling underneath the window frame of Mr Rogers' classroom with Cathy, our arthritic teaching assistant, incredulously shuffling several metres behind us. Now I'm not advocating you follow this example (my own approach to reverse psychology has become more subtle in the years since then) but I'd never seen those boys so enthusiastic about studying poetry, even in the face of a howling gale. And even Mr Rogers agreed that it was a good result when I told him about it later.

More recently, in my role as a senior leader, a concerned colleague came to report to me that the Year 11 students planned to mark their last day of school by ordering Domino's Pizza at lunchtime (there is a strange paranoia that descends upon some schools around this time of year). Buoyed by the fact that, as far as acts of rebellion go, this was pretty tame and cautioned by the horror stories I'd heard relating to last-day shenanigans at other schools, I told the colleague to 'leave it with me' and then promptly did nothing. The students enjoyed their mischief and got one over the teachers by enjoying a surreptitious pizza and the day went off incident free. *Everyone won.*

These are one-off examples but it is an approach that can work (if you know your group well enough) so next time you've got 9B for chemistry at 2pm on a Thursday afternoon, why not say to them, 'We're not supposed to, but I really fancy doing an experiment today' and see whether their level of enthusiasm for this *mischief* is amplified.

'Seek first to understand, then to be understood'

I've lifted this line shamelessly from Stephen R Covey but, of his *Seven Habits of Highly Effective People*, it's the precept that – for me at least – is the most important.

Children are – like all people – an elaborate compound of their emotions, their experiences and their environment. Unlike adults, however, they are not as adept at moderating (or making sense of) this mishmash of emotions and often the whole volatile concoction can explode. Your job, as a teacher and/or pastoral leader, is to take all this into account (often while displaying the patience of Job) and use this information to guide you when working with each young person.

Children are – like all people –an elaborate compound of their emotions, their experiences and their environment.

This personalised level of care relies upon knowledge and, as a subject teacher who might only see Pupil X for an hour per week, you might not necessarily have this information readily available. Nonetheless, it's your job to find it. The student's head of house/year or form tutor should be the go-to person and should be able to provide the contextual information which will help you to make sense of this puzzle. Once you have this information, it's important that you treat it with the same discretion that you'd like your own sensitive personal details to be handled with and you can then use it to inform the way that you interact with the young person in your care.

For instance, if the young person lives in a home dominated by aggressive males, it might be expedient to think carefully about the way you interact with them in order to avoid any potential emotional triggers. In this situation, the last thing you want to bear even a passing resemblance to is an *aggressive male*. Similarly, if a child has lost a parent or has experienced neglect, their negative behaviour may in fact require love and care rather than firmness and admonishment.

Whatever the variables happen to be, the more you understand the students' behaviours and the emotions and history that underpin them, the better equipped you are to manage them.

Teamwork makes the dream work

If there's one thing that irks me as a teacher it's when senior leaders constantly seek to draw analogies from sport to suit any situation, as if all of life's many other pursuits are somehow secondary replicants of what happens on a sports field. I'm sports mad myself and I even draw on a few sporting analogies in this book but, whenever I hear the fateful words 'sport can teach us lots of lessons about life' at the start of an assembly or at a presentation evening, I immediately scan the room looking for the eyes glazing over on the faces of the many children for whom sport holds no interest at all and whose primary association with physical activity may actually amount to ritual humiliation and guaranteed failure during PE lessons.

Having said all that, one lesson that sport can teach us about life is the importance of establishing a strong dynamic and a positive shared culture within the team. In our case, the *team* is the class and, although some of your aims may be consistent, the culture and identity of the team has to be shaped by the individuals in front of you and they have to be values and ideals that they can buy into.

Positive affirmation can play a huge part in this process. If you've got a Year 10 class with a heavy distribution of 'band A' students, it can be helpful to apply a positive label in the hope of it developing into a self-fulfilling prophecy ('This is one of the most potentially able classes I've taught. If we all work hard and support each other, we can achieve anything'). I've seen this happen with a class made up predominantly of high flyers where they collectively decided that they would all aim for a grade A (or above) and the collective ethos was to 'work hard and aim high'. Unsurprisingly, the high flyers did just that but the really remarkable thing was, even some of the students whose baseline assessment scores did not indicate a similar level of academic aptitude bought into the same shared ethos and achieved similar results. Perhaps this suggests that what the mind believes, it truly can achieve!

There is still a place for team building as long as the focus is on input rather than outcome.

This shared culture may well have played a part in the success of this particular group but it's not one that can be parachuted into any given class. Nonetheless, a shared dynamic can be equally powerful if it's carefully considered. For a middle set group, defiance might be a stronger motivating emotion ('Let's see if we can outdo set one!'), while for a less able and potentially less confident group the shared triggers might be even more bespoke.

What's important is that, while 'working hard and aiming high' can be positive motivators that the whole class can buy into, you have to be mindful of introducing a toxic, and overly competitive, dynamic to your class. Being able to tell a supposedly lower ability group that they're 'working really hard and smashing their targets' can be incredibly motivating and empowering but it has to be tempered by the fact that the ultimate goal is to do the best you can as an individual.

Effective teaching can be predicated on having a thorough knowledge of what makes each of the individuals you work with tick but, although they will each be judged on their individual performances (at least in terms of external exams), there is still a place for team building and, as long as the focus is on input rather than outcome and the culture reflects the identity of the students who make up the group, it can be an effective tool.

Respect is more sustainable than fear

As a teacher (and an adult) you walk into a classroom with a number of distinct and in-built advantages at your disposal. Sure, you may be outnumbered 30-1, but you have the benefit of your years of experience, your status and the fact that the rules of the school ultimately dictate that your word is final. For a lot of teachers there's also the added benefit that, as well as wielding this institutional authority, they're also physically bigger and probably louder too. It's almost understandable therefore that some colleagues adopt the persona of *scary teacher* in order to keep their classes in check – but it's not a mantle I've ever been tempted to assume.

As an NQT, I can remember a senior colleague observing one of my lessons and remarking disappointedly, 'You're a big lad, you play rugby, I thought you'd be much more scary!' That same colleague then regaled me proudly with his foolproof method of making transgressing students cry (if you're curious as to what this involved, I won't be sharing his suggested technique and this probably isn't the book for you) and I decided there and then that my approach to behaviour management was going to be very different to his.

Noise and fear are like antibiotics; after you've been using them for a while they lose their efficacy.

Rather than accentuate my physical size as a means to assert control, I often find it more helpful to mitigate it in order to be less imposing and more approachable (for example, choosing to sit down in order to communicate with a student at eye level). Sure, there may be times where *controlled pantomime* is needed and, consequently, the shoulders come back and the voice is raised but these moments of shock and awe should only be used sparingly in order to hammer home an important point or emphasise that a non-negotiable line has been breached (for me, that usually involves bullying). But, as I hope I made clear earlier, noise and fear are like antibiotics; after you've been using them for a while they lose their efficacy and you'll need a more effective remedy. Respect, on the other hand, is something that – once earned – is far more valued and, as far as behaviour management is concerned, is effective for much longer.

When you exploit an imbalance of power in order to assume control, it can be effective but it looks and sounds a lot like a form of bullying and that's not a behaviour type that, as teachers, we should be seeking to model. Moreover, if we can choose instead to build relationships based on trust and mutual respect, the results are often more positive and long lasting.

As a lifelong Manchester United fan, it might not surprise you to learn that I often highlight the career of José Mourinho when citing examples of poor leadership. It's true that 'The Special One' has achieved incredible success throughout his career but he's never been able to sustain that success in any one place for any length of time. For me, the reasons for that are simple. Firstly, he has always had the means at his disposal to disregard players who he doesn't like the look of and select ready-made alternatives, rather than having to take the time to improve the individuals already at the club. As a teacher, that's not a luxury you're likely to have at your disposal – nor should it be one that you desire.

Success is never permanent and, if you're the type of 'leader' who chooses to rule by fear, neither is your authority.

Secondly, Mourinho has always struck me as a leader who has ruled by fear. Not unlike one or two headteachers I've come across, he tends to select (often arbitrarily) one or two 'whipping boys' and always has a tendency to publicly berate his players while, at the same time, tacitly attributing their successes to his own 'genius'. As a result, other players tend to perform partly because they fear assuming the mantle of the whipping boy themselves. However many trophies he may have accrued, that's not a 'leadership style' I'd be particularly keen to adopt myself.

Mourinho also relies on another form of fear: FOMO. When things are going well there is undoubtedly a 'fear of missing out' among Mourinho's players; everybody wants to be part of a winning team so, when success is forthcoming, players are willing to tolerate Mourinho's idiosyncrasies and his unpleasantness. The problem is that, no matter how hard you work, success is never a given and, if you're the type of 'leader' who chooses to rule by fear, neither is your authority. When the chips are down, fear is no longer a trait that will control those around you and instead you're left reliant on more positive (and sustainable) values such as respect and loyalty. History shows that those leaders who choose to lead by fear often meet a premature and grisly end once those they have oppressed sense a hint of weakness. Sadly, it still seems that one or two 'leaders' within our profession don't have a grasp of this history.

CHAPTER 5:

Understanding the power of your interactions

In an age where parents are sometimes unwilling, unable or simply ill-equipped to provide the formative life lessons that their children require and – frighteningly – kids are increasingly looking to YouTubers, 'influencers' and reality TV stars for guidance and inspiration, the role of the teacher has never been more important. As well as teaching our chosen subjects, hitting increasingly taxing targets, and acting as social workers, counsellors and surrogate parents, we are also role models – perhaps the only positive role models that many children have access to.

Many children spend more time with their teachers than they do with their parents and, even where this is not the case, not all parents are capable of acting as role models. As such, teachers are in a position of tremendous power and responsibility – and there is nowhere that this power and responsibility needs to be more carefully applied than in our use of language. The words and phrases we choose are more powerful than we can possibly imagine. They can raise children up, inspire and empower them or they can diminish, disenfranchise and demoralise. In either case, the results can be long-lasting, and therefore we need to choose our words carefully, consider their potential effects and – hopefully – use the power of our language as a force for good.

The words and phrases we choose are more
powerful than we can possibly imagine.

Having attended school during a slightly less enlightened age, I have experienced both edges of this sword myself and understand that the words uttered by those in positions of authority can break chains but also inflict deep and long-lasting wounds.

Thankfully, things have moved on from those times when a head of year could prod a 13-year-old classmate of mine in the chest and refer to him as 'dross' and 'low-life' while informing him that he'll 'never amount to anything!' 30 years on, it still horrifies me that an experienced English teacher could daub 'Carl Fletcher's alternative spellings' on the chalkboard before spending the next five minutes publicly humiliating a child whose only crime was not being able to spell particularly well. I'd like to hope that these examples are as anachronistic as they are shocking but it would be naive to think that there aren't still teachers in our midst who are prone to leveraging insults and humiliation as a form of classroom control. There should be no place for these individuals in our profession but we all have to strive to be better too.

Beware of *worms*

When assessing the potential impact of a teacher's choice of language, it's always worth invoking the Peter Parker principle: 'With great power there must also come great responsibility.'

Too often, however, some of our colleagues are guilty (often inadvertently) of disregarding this maxim and this can cause disengagement in the short term and demoralisation and insecurity that can last a lifetime. I often liken these misjudged (and occasionally malicious) utterances to worms or parasites. The person issuing them can often see them as small, innocuous and easily forgotten; for the recipient, however, these words burrow deep, grow to a crippling size and, if never treated, can cause lifelong damage.

I'm inclined to believe that we're all intrinsically good so, when these *worms* are released, I prefer to put it down to poor judgement rather than virulence. But we do all need to be mindful of both the words we choose and the impact they can have.

At a most basic level, this has to include avoiding attributing negativity towards an individual and instead focusing any sense of disappointment towards negative behaviour and choices. A short phrase such as 'You're lazy' or 'You're naughty' or even 'Your handwriting is terrible' may be an ill-judged, throwaway remark but they each have the power to demoralise, disengage and – particularly where an individual is predisposed to poor self-esteem – can unleash a highly negative self-fulfilling prophecy.

Moreover, each of those phrases can be easily exchanged for something like 'You need to work harder' or 'I'm really disappointed with the choice you made there' or 'Let's work together to improve your handwriting.' This may sound like little more than semantics but, in each of these examples, you are exchanging a negative label directed at the individual for formative feedback about their behaviour/choices, while also offering support and a more positive (and achievable) alternative.

The power of your words is heightened because you have chosen an occupation where your language choices really matter – particularly to the children you teach. Once you're fully aware of the power of those words, why would you use this power as anything other than a force for good?

Try to plant *positive worms*

I may be in need of a more apt metaphor here but it's always struck me that, if those worms that we can occasionally unleash can cause so much damage, why don't we spend more time applying the same logic in reverse? The answer, in my opinion, is simple: *positive worms* can have just as transformative and long-lasting an impact as their malicious cousins.

Once we've invested in relationships and earned the trust that we discussed earlier, we are imbued with the power to not only enhance someone's self-esteem in the short term but also (potentially) change their lives for the better. All we have to do is open our mouths, choose the right words and convince the recipient to take them on board (this last bit is often the hardest part as people tend to be predisposed to accept the negative labels that are cast upon them yet far more reluctant to embrace positive feedback).

The key to this – as is often the case – is honesty. If you tell a child 'You're lazy' they're often inclined to conclude 'If that's what you think I am, that's what I might as well be.' Unfortunately, the reverse doesn't quite work out. Telling a student 'You're an incredible scientist' may – if you're lucky – bring about a brief confidence boost but, unless it's grounded in truth, the positive effects will be fleeting.

This is another occasion where a teacher's ability to find those shards of gold in each individual really comes to the fore. Where a student displays a flair for say, poetry, it should be as easy for the teacher to issue this epithet as it is for the recipient to accept it. But where an individual has less obvious aptitude for a particular skill/subject area our *gold-mining* skills need to be a little more finely tuned. The answer to this conundrum is to return to one of the maxims that lies at the heart of all good teaching: focus your praise on the process, rather than the outcome.

Focus your praise on the process,
rather than the outcome.

If Richard struggles at physics and, no matter how hard he works, may never achieve a creditable grade for the subject in an external examination, it's still possible to find the *gold* in this situation and to provide the kind of positive affirmation that he can apply to those areas where he is more able, while also imbuing him with a positive label that he can carry throughout his life.

A few well-chosen sentences can be incredibly powerful: 'Richard, the thing that always impresses me about you is that, no matter how difficult you find something, you never give up and always do everything you can to get the job done. That's an incredible quality that I know will take you far in life.' Suddenly, a few simple words have transformed Richard's lack of aptitude for physics into a positive (and potentially empowering) statement about his future career prospects. It's also a reminder that sometimes the reach of our impact as teachers travels well beyond our chosen subject areas.

Success comes in all shapes and sizes

It's always worth remembering that, as teachers, we may have followed a path that is very different to that of the students we teach. Many of us will have possessed a natural aptitude towards academia; most of us will have enjoyed school; few of us will have felt inclined to liken the education system to a running race that we've been forced into with both of our legs tied together. For many of our students the reverse is true.

For those particular students the curriculum we deliver and the language it arrives wrapped up in is alien and holds no relevance to them or their lives. Some may well work hard but – even with all the support we offer – are consigned to failure in a system that still casts many children as square pegs that we spend around 15 years trying to force into round holes. These kids are generally part of the unfortunate minority that some schools write off as collateral damage while totting up their attainment figures. The question is whether those schools still have a responsibility to direct those youngsters towards their next destination filled with confidence, self-belief and purpose.

Sadly, my experience is that this is not always the case. Too many young people leave our education system broken, directionless and disenchanted, rather than uplifted and empowered. For the sake of our society, and for the children these young people go on to have themselves, we need that to change.

As teachers, that means providing more empowerment and encouragement to those youngsters who aren't stereotypically academic. There's a wider discussion to be had about the need for more effective vocational pathways and a less superficial approach to careers guidance but, for our part, we need to pick up some of the slack by instilling confidence, unearthing nascent talent and trying to provide direction and guidance.

Unfortunately, as teachers, our perception of what success looks like is often framed through the narrow prism of having attended university and found a respectable white-collar job.

One thing we must all endeavour to avoid is imposing our own middle-class values upon the children we teach. Phrases like 'If you don't pass your exams, you'll end up working at McDonalds' may be intended to motivate but they can often have the entirely opposite effect. Not only do they belittle jobs that don't fit our own middle-class ideals of what success looks like but they also heighten the pressure already associated with formal examinations. The cold, hard truth is that some children won't perform well academically – no matter how hard they work or how much support we are able to put in place. With that in mind, it's far better to choose your words carefully and link input and outcome in more generic terms ('If you work hard now, you'll have far more choices open to you later in life').

Unfortunately, as teachers, our perception of what success looks like is often framed through the narrow prism of having attended university and found a respectable white-collar job. The cold facts are that around half the population doesn't attend university and we have a moral duty to prepare these kids for a rewarding life that doesn't happen to follow a traditional academic route. Given the pressure we face in guiding our students through public examinations, it's understandable that such a narrow world view is ingrained in our profession. But we have to look beyond that and see that our remit lies well beyond steering children over the right side of an arbitrary academic line; our job is to lead children through an often flawed education system that only values and rewards a narrow set of attributes and hopefully bring them out at the other end with their confidence enhanced and with a clear sense of purpose.

Our job is to guide children through an often flawed education system that only values and rewards a narrow set of attributes.

Tom may be teetering on the precipice of grade 3-4 for maths but we can't reinforce the perception that, even if he tries as hard as he can but still finds himself on the wrong side of the line, he is deemed a failure. If we propagate that particular myth, how can we encourage Tom to work hard in the first place? Or do our own narrow parameters simply guide Tom down the well-worn path of choosing to be the badly behaved kid rather than being seen as the 'thick kid'. Too many *Toms* feel compelled (often through embarrassment and shame) to tread this particular path and, once they're on it, it's a path that seldom leads to a positive perception of education or a fulfilling life beyond school. Once that negative perception becomes hardwired, the risk is that the damage doesn't just afflict Tom; its limiting impact becomes generational.

Our job is to support the many *Toms* who are out there; help them to reach their academic potential (whatever the ceiling for that happens to be) but also to guide them to a destination in life where they can achieve their own success, gain fulfilment and make a positive contribution to society. To look at it another way, Jeremy may well write beautifully crafted essays, achieve grade 9s across the board and earn a place at Oxbridge, but would you really want to call him if your boiler was on the blink? Success comes in all shapes and sizes.

Your success as a teacher is partly dependent on how well you prepare the children in your care for an increasingly challenging and unforgiving world.

Your words are so powerful and transformative. *Choose them well.*

CHAPTER 6:
Building successful home–school partnerships

So you've probably caught the drift by now that much of what's being advocated here revolves around taking the time to build solid, trust-based relationships but there's one set of important constituents of the school community who are sometimes overlooked, marginalised and (occasionally) disrespected: the parents.

Too often, parents are kept out of the loop, talked down to and only contacted when things have unravelled completely. Yet if you invest the time needed to build an effective partnership from the get-go, maintain regular contact (rather than waiting for things to go wrong) and treat them as equal partners in the business of getting the best out of your students, then parents can be your most valuable allies.

Before we explain how to build these relationships, however, along with the immense dividends they can yield, it's probably time to venture into another bout of myth-busting. So here goes: there is no such thing as a *demanding parent*. If you have kids of your own you will understand that nothing is too good for your children and, if their needs are not being sufficiently met, you will fight tooth and nail and bang on any door necessary in order to have the situation rectified. Once you put yourself in the shoes of the parent, it's much easier to flip this particular script and to exchange the adjective in the noun phrase 'demanding parent' from *demanding* to *devoted*. Ultimately, we should be grateful that we have parents who care (particularly when indifference and neglect are sadly so prevalent) and, if we're smart, we can utilise this engagement to benefit everyone – even if we have to work hard to encourage some parents to toe the line between care and combativeness.

> *There is no such thing as a 'demanding parent' – they're devoted parents who need to be encouraged to toe the line between care and combativeness.*

This willingness to battle for your offspring is particularly acute when the child concerned has special educational needs. In these instances we should be full of admiration for the 'tiger mums' (and dads) who are so fierce in the protection of their cubs. I can remember one particular occasion when the mother of an autistic child was causing consternation among some of my colleagues due to her escalating demands.

'You'll never believe what Mrs Smith wants now,' bemoaned a particularly committed but nonetheless frazzled former colleague of mine.

'What?'

'She's only decided that Peter needs someone to mentor him for an hour a week because he's nervous about going to university. How am I supposed to staff that? We're completely overstretched as it is!'

After giving it a couple of seconds' thought, I replied, 'Don't worry, I'll do it.'

I didn't actually have the time or the capacity myself but I knew that, if I could find that time from somewhere, it would be a weight off my colleague's shoulders and of benefit to the student. As it turned out, that stolen hour per week was time that I grew to treasure and gave me the opportunity to witness a shy, bewildered boy grow into a confident, impressive young man. Almost as importantly, the willingness to *go the extra mile* for a child who required additional input was a huge weight off the mind of this particular tiger mum and cemented a rock-solid home–school partnership that endured for many years afterwards.

This is one of many examples of successful home–school partnerships that I have been able to utilise over the years, with each one yielding a range of benefits – both for the child concerned and for the wider school community (those parents who are onside also tend to end up being the first ones to volunteer to help around school and can often be relied upon as an 'early warning system' when trouble is looming on the horizon).

From personal experience, I've never been as grateful for having invested the time into building these strong partnerships as I was during the Covid lockdown. Having our classes working from home, with a range of other potential distractions at their disposal, was a nightmare for many of us. But my army of tiger mums (and tiger dads) was priceless and I always knew that a quick email saying, 'Tell your Jack to get off his PlayStation and log onto my lesson!' would almost always yield the result I required.

Effective partnerships such as this don't emerge by chance, however, and they don't happen overnight but I'll try to outline below some simple steps towards developing these relationships:

1. **Every second you invest will be paid back tenfold.** This is the mentality you need to adopt from the word go if you're going to make this work. You may be busy, you may be stressed, you may have a thousand competing priorities that all appear to trump the desire to pick up the phone or draft an email, but try to find the time: it'll be worth it in the long run.
2. **Begin the process as soon as possible.** Don't wait; find an excuse, even if it's just to introduce yourself as Siobhan's new French teacher. This opening gambit may only be generic but, as long as you add some form of personalisation and avoid any embarrassing faux pas (e.g. mixing up the pronouns in an email you'll be adapting for the whole class), it can initiate a dialogue and lay the foundations for a relationship that can prove invaluable in the long run.
3. **Don't worry about what your colleagues are doing.** The fact that many of them won't see the importance of establishing contact at this early stage actually works in your favour. Your early engagement and willingness to go beyond normal expectations marks you out as

different and will earn you brownie points that you may well need to cash in later.

4. **Try to make the first contact a positive one.** We're back – as always – to the maxim of 'catching them being good' but it's never more important than in this particular context. Parents are conditioned to only expect a call from school when things have gone awry. The fact that you've taken the time to get in touch to relay some positive news will therefore be a welcome surprise and will again mark you out as being a teacher who is committed and cares. The long-term benefits will also be important here; there may well come a time when you find it necessary to call with less positive news (missing homework, poor behaviour in class, etc) and where a parent's stock response might well be inclined towards the defensive (this is their little angel you're calling about!) and where the child might well pull out the 'he/she's always picking on me' card. In this situation, the fact that you've already invested the time to relay positive news in the past, not only draws down some of the parental barriers but also renders the child's defence redundant.

5. **Make it clear that you care.** It's not rocket science but, just as the last chapter outlined how important it is for children to feel liked and valued by their teachers, the same applies to parents too. It's important for them to know that you like their child, value them, treat them fairly, see their potential and understand each of their quirks and peccadilloes. That kind of knowledge and understanding builds trust – not least in the fact that, in the parents' eyes, their child's education is in safe hands.

6. **Establish an open door policy.** It always baffles me why so many schools choose to put so many barriers in between teachers and parents; too few schools even take the simple step of ensuring that each teacher's email address is easily located on the school website. Quite why this apparent schism exists is beyond me but you should do all you can to tear these barriers down. My advice is to spell out an open door policy whereby, if a parent needs anything or is unsure about something, they only need ask. Contrary to the myth of the demanding parent, most parents won't actually feel compelled to take you up on this but the fact that the offer is there is reassuring and will cement the relationship.

7. **Be pre-emptive.** Once you've initiated contact, forged the relationship and established that your door is always open, the next ground rule to introduce is this: never allow a minor issue to fester and become a big problem. It sounds simple (and it is!) but most of the minor queries, issues and (occasionally) complaints that parents have can be quickly addressed, without the need for escalation or intervention. It's through the instances where 'I didn't want to trouble you' that bigger problems emerge and, for the time it takes to respond promptly to an email, why not grasp the opportunity to squash that potential problem before it takes root?

Good schools will, of course, enshrine much of this good practice in their routines and expectations but – in the absence of this – there's nothing to stop you adopting any of these approaches yourself. I can't guarantee that it will make you bullet-proof from any difficult situations involving parents. Some people are just unreasonable and occasionally even unpleasant but your proactiveness will help to bring the cooperative majority onside and will mitigate any potential problems with the more difficult minority.

Moreover, just as educational logic abounds with a number of prevalent myths, parents aren't short of some of their own either. My favourite trope (which is one of the most common) goes along the lines of, 'My Gavin is no angel but one thing he isn't is a liar!'

Where to start with this whopper? OK, first up, all kids are liars when it suits them. I've got two of my own at home and they're most certainly not angels but they are most definitely liars. Given the choice between being told off and sacrificing access to their technology or accepting responsibility for their actions, kids will lie. It's in their DNA.

> *All kids will lie when it suits them. I've got two of my own at home and they're certainly not angels but they definitely are liars.*

Even *good kids* will lie occasionally. In fact, on the occasions where they do get something wrong, they're almost more likely to lie than their more recidivist peers who (if you follow the advice outlined elsewhere in this book) are more *au fait* with the notion that, if you do something wrong, the best response is to own up and fix it.

I can remember a particular occasion when a student made a *really* serious boo-boo. A colleague of mine carried out the most thorough investigation into the incident possible but, when the identity of the culprit was established, was shocked to learn that it was the most angelic individual imaginable, someone who you would never have dreamt could be capable of an indiscretion of this nature. Faced with overwhelming evidence, the young person concerned had little choice but to own up to his guilt immediately. The fun started when he got home, however.

Faced with an angry parent, the young man suddenly decided to change his story and claimed that he'd only confessed because he'd felt pressured into doing so by the member of staff carrying out the investigation. This prompted a very angry response from a normally supportive parent who kicked things off with a variation on a well-worn theme: 'Our Ryan is a good lad. We understand that he's not a complete angel but one thing we do know is that he never tells lies.'

Now 'our Ryan' was indeed a good lad and, contrary to what his dad had said, he usually was pretty angelic but, as we've already established, all kids will lie when it's expedient to do so. Nevertheless, out of respect for both the truth and the parents' usually supportive stance, I agreed to reinvestigate the issue myself and report back to them once I'd got to the bottom of things.

First of all, I went back to my colleague who confirmed that no coercion tactics had been used to elicit the original confession. I then went back and reinterviewed each of the original witnesses in order to establish a clear timeline and, once complete, all of the evidence pointed unequivocally towards the same thing: 'Our Ryan' was bang to rights.

Once presented with the facts again, the young man paused briefly and then politely and contritely reconfirmed that he was indeed the guilty party. This still begged the question, 'Why did you lie when you got home?' The answer was simple, illuminating and naively understandable: 'Because I don't usually get in trouble and I didn't want my parents to be disappointed.'

All kids 'tell fibs'. *At least some of the time.*

CHAPTER 7:

Making parents' evenings and school reports count

As the last chapter should have made clear, effective home–school partnerships are absolutely essential, but in many schools you're going to have to do a lot of the legwork yourself as the importance of these relationships isn't underpinned by the policies or routines that have been put in place. The one notable exception that you will find in all schools is the provision of parents' evenings and school reports.

The precise implementation of both of these things and the overall effectiveness of them will vary from school to school. But every school will have them. Regardless of how effectively the management of your school implements either of these things, your job is to make them work for you.

We'll look at different ways to make both parents' evenings and school reports as effective as possible in a moment but, before we do so, here is a selection of crucial maxims that cut across them both:

1. **Never 'premiere' bad news for the first time in a report or at a parents' evening.** If Aleesha is failing at maths, has not been submitting homework or has been behaving appallingly, her parents have every right to ask, 'Why have you waited until now to tell us?' You'll have paved the way for a difficult conversation and, what's more, they'll have a fair point! Always make sure that you pre-empt these difficult situations by maintaining the vital home–school contact we discussed earlier and delivering bad news in a more timely fashion.

2. **Remember, you are writing/talking about someone's child!** This might sound obvious but I've read some draft reports and had to intervene on one or two parents' evening consultations that have amounted to little more than sustained character assassinations and have (understandably) provoked an angry response from parents (which can be particularly problematic at a parents' evening). Ali may well be the bane of your life and might be a constant source of disruption but he is also – almost certainly – the apple of Mr and Mrs Hussain's eye so please bear that in mind before you start typing/talking.

3. **Don't ignore the elephant in the room.** Inevitably, even if it shouldn't come out of the blue, you will need to factor some bad news into either a report or a parents' evening consultation. Don't shy away from it. I've seen too many examples of teachers (particularly in KS4/5) telling parents what they want to hear, rather than what they need to hear and then being left with a heap of explaining to do when the actual results land and present a far less rosy picture than the one you've been painting. Don't fall into this trap; address the areas of concern, rather than hoping they'll go away.

4. **Always lead on a positive.** It's much easier to address those areas of concern if you follow the teachers' mantra and try to balance things out with some positive feedback. This may again necessitate some 'sifting for gold among the muck' on your part but a wholly negative report/consultation is likely to achieve nothing other than alienating the parent and cementing the perception that you simply don't like the child. Meanwhile, for the actual student, constant, unmitigated criticism quickly becomes white noise and only serves to disengage.

5. **Always make it clear that you know the child.** This might seem superfluous to those of you with tunnel vision where your subject is concerned – particularly when word counts and time limits come into play – but make sure you devote at least some time to making it abundantly clear that you know (and value) the child. Adding this context, whether through the written word or a face-to-face consultation, prevents whatever feedback you provide from being soulless and dry and signals to the parent that you are not the distant, unapproachable ogre that they may have been warned about but

are, in fact, someone who knows their child, cares about them and is committed to seeing them do well. As ever, the language you choose here is critical and needs to be carefully crafted and considered.

6. **Don't blind them with science.** This bit really comes down to understanding your audience. The person either sitting opposite you or sitting at home reading their child's report is probably not a grammarian or a physicist and their last interaction with the geography syllabus was probably back during their own school days. You have to think about what you aim to achieve here: do you want to amaze them with your subject knowledge? Or do you want to reinforce current good performance or effect positive change? If it's the latter then you'd be best advised to use layman's terms where possible and to frame your message in a manner that will achieve that desired response. That doesn't mean *dumbing things down* but it does involve giving careful consideration to your use of language, register and tone and may also require you to adapt your approach for different parents (just as you would their children).

7. **Don't overload with data.** Data is important; it's essential that you provide an accurate and timely gauge of both performance and potential. However, context is everything and, unless you thoroughly and carefully contextualise these raw numbers, in relation to targets, attainment and capability, your sharing of them can actually do far more harm than good. For example, Kara may be busting a gut and confounding her baseline scores to work at a grade 5 but her ambitious parents may not understand the GCSE marking framework and might look at 5 (out of a possible 9 grades) as tantamount to failure. The manner in which you present this data (particularly at parents' evenings) is also critical and has the potential to be misinterpreted or misrepresented. For instance, your message that 'Christopher is capable of achieving a grade 7' can quickly be subverted to 'You told us that Christopher would get a grade 7!' by the time results day rolls around.

8. **Always make sure that targets are clear, achievable and understood.** This last bit is all important as, without it, the whole venture can be a bit of a pointless exercise. For parents' evenings and reports the ultimate aim has to be to provide (and reinforce) formative feedback. For this to be worthwhile, the feedback needs to be easily understood,

relevant to the child and achievable. If it's not or if it's generic (e.g. 'Revise more') then you're probably wasting your energy/breath.

Although both written reports and face-to-face consultations share many similar aims (see above), there are, of course, distinct differences that need to be taken into account in order to maximise the impact of both opportunities and to prevent either from amounting to little more than a time-consuming, box-ticking exercise.

School reports

The term 'school report' is a pretty generic name for a document that can come in a whole range of different shapes, sizes, formats and colours and can be distributed with varying degrees of regularity.

Some schools still insist on a lengthy written report for each subject – often mistaking quantity of words typed for quality of message delivered – while others virtually eschew the written word completely and instead opt for colour-coded tables, with lots of data to scan across but little in the way of warmth, personality or context.

Personally, I'm not particularly fond of either format. In terms of written comments, less can often equal more and it's far better to deliver clear, concise and personalised feedback, than offer rambling prose which long overstays its welcome and is often reliant on generic 'super sentences'.

Speaking as a parent, the brightly coloured 'Tetris grids' are no more appealing, can feel even more soulless and generic and are often only rescued by the brief contextual comments that tend to be appended upon them by the form tutor or head of year.

The frequency of reports can also vary from school to school. Some schools favour the little and often approach of a 'data report' delivered every half term (with provision for a more detailed report at the end of the year). The logic behind this is that it provides parents with a regular update of their child's attainment in relation to their prescribed targets. The potential flaw here is that, as was pointed out earlier, not all parents have a thorough understanding of this data and, when presented without context, it can often lead to misunderstanding and set hares racing that the teaching staff will then struggle to round up again.

When presented without context, data can often lead to misunderstanding.

At the opposite end of the scale, other (often more traditional) schools prefer to present a wordier tome on an annual basis, the flaws of which I have already alluded to elsewhere.

For the purpose of providing you with useful direction, I'm going to assume that the majority of readers will work at schools that employ the happy medium of a report that consists of data relating to attainment, target grades, effort/application, concise individualised comments/feedback and personalised targets.

Applying an assumed word count of 100 words or fewer per section, I'll give you a potential approach to structuring both your comments and your targets, try to steer you away from a few common errors and also supply you with examples of good and bad report writing.

Things to avoid in your reports:

1. Generic copy and paste sentences.
2. Embarrassing errors prompted by copying generic sentences (e.g. using the wrong name/pronouns).
3. Over-reliance upon generic 'super sentences' that start with things like 'This year we have been studying...' and are filled with superfluous information.
4. Diatribes of unadulterated negativity.
5. Negative personal comments/labels (remember, choose your words carefully!).

6. Ill-advised comments that create the impression that your classroom is a haven for negative behaviour.
7. Rambling/nebulous targets.
8. Generic targets that are neither personal, helpful or particularly easy to assess (e.g. 'Work harder' or 'Revise more').

Things to include in your reports:

1. Personalised comments that provide colour and warmth, and demonstrate that you know the child and value their presence in your class.
2. Useful feedback which contextualises the data in relation to the individual student's aptitude, input and potential.
3. Positive comments (your job is to find them) that balance out any necessary negativity, and provide grounds for optimism and a path towards improvement.
4. Examples of areas of the curriculum/specific pieces of work which the student has enjoyed or performed well in.
5. Examples where some of the qualities that the student has demonstrated could prove to be useful in life (e.g. 'Etta's determination and attention to detail will make her very employable when she's older').
6. Closing comments that briefly summarise the body of the report and provide encouragement for the future.
7. Bullet point targets which are concise, personalised, easily assimilated and actionable.

Now let's look at three reports for the same student and see which examples of good and bad practice we can identify.

REPORT 1

Comments:
Imaya enjoys PE and has attended netball training regularly this year. She arrives on time to lessons and usually has the correct kit. This year we have been focusing on cross-country running, invasion games and gymnastics. Imaya has performed well in all activities and demonstrated a positive attitude. Well done, Imaya.

Targets:
She/he should exercise regularly and aim to maintain a balanced diet. Practice ball skills and aim to go for a run/brisk walk at least twice per week. Joining a local sports club will also help improve your performance in team sports.

Although the overall content of this report is OK, it has a feeling of being cold and generic. There are tell-tale signs that super sentences have been used, including the copied and pasted summary of the programme that the class has been completing (sentence 3). There is little sense of the teacher knowing or valuing the student as an individual and even the personalised comments come across as cold and slightly clinical.

The targets seem vague and generic and the fact that they are prefaced by 'she/he' is a clear indicator that they have been copied and pasted and are identical to other reports issued in the class (a fact likely to be verified if Imaya's mum/dad speaks to any of the other parents).

REPORT 2

Comments:
Imaia (sic) does not appear to enjoy art and often lacks focus during lessons.

In art this year we have been studying Cubism, 3D modelling, portraiture and caricature.

Imaia can use a pencil and choose colours. She has had a reasonable year and may consider art as an option in Year 10.

Targets:
Carry a sketch book around with you and practise drawing when you can. Try to focus on your own work rather than being dragged off task by other disruptive influences within the class.

In truth, this report is a bit of a mess and the fact that the teacher appears to have misspelt the student's name is likely to alienate the parents even more than the negative opening. Again, the report is fleshed out by a brief summary of the topics covered this year and, although the teacher does allude to skills developed in the final paragraph, the comments are vague and lack context. The closing comments, alluding to the potential of the student selecting art as a GCSE option, are a little optimistic given the negative nature of the report.

The targets are equally vague and generic and the closing comments relating to the student are again negative and actually imply a prevalence of poor behaviour and disengagement within the class.

REPORT 3

Comments:
Imaya has had a really encouraging year in history and often makes telling contributions to class discussions. Although she struggled to engage with the topic of Industrial Britain, she has been fascinated by our recent exploration of the British Empire and has been inspired to produce some much-improved written work. Imaya has the potential to be a capable historian if she can improve the detail of her written responses and apply a more consistent approach to learning.

Targets:
- Make sure you proofread your extended answers carefully in order to ensure that your ideas are clearly expressed.
- Try to justify your ideas in more detail, citing accurate historical examples.
- Where possible, explore different interpretations of historic events and assess the validity of available evidence.

There's a real contrast between this report and the two that precede it. The teacher wisely leads on a positive and focuses their comments on the specific area in which the individual student has demonstrated the most promise. Areas of underperformance, where improvement is required, are highlighted but they have been presented in a more sensitive manner, with positive elements being used effectively as a counterbalance. The summary at the end of the comments offers both encouragement and direction, while the targets have clearly been personalised and are easily assimilated thanks to both the use of bullet points and the clarity of language employed.

Writing reports effectively is a skill that all teachers can – and should – be capable of developing. You don't need a flair for florid prose or creative fiction. All you do need is a knowledge of your students, an understanding of the impact of your language choices and a positive outlook. If you employ these three things, report writing can actually be a rewarding and impactful activity, rather than a time-consuming and potentially damaging exercise.

Parents' evenings

There was a time when parents' evenings were a broadly similar affair across most schools (in both the state and independent sectors) across the country. The Covid-19 pandemic has changed all that. 18 months ago all but the most tech-savvy among us would have been nonplussed by the prospect of meeting up on Zoom or Teams. Yet here we are and, for the time being at least, remote parents' evenings are part of our *new normal.*

Many schools will undoubtedly be looking at how seamlessly they have adapted to this implementation of technology and questioning whether or not we should revert back to the old way of doing things at all. That's a question for later, however, and – whether you're sitting two feet away from parents in a crowded hall or engaging with them via a laptop – the overall concept of parents' evening remains largely the same.

One of the most crucial tenets behind any worthwhile parents' evening is this: it's not a time for revelations but it is an opportunity for affirmation, motivation and clarification.

Parents' evenings are not a time for revelations but they are an opportunity for affirmation, motivation and clarification.

If there are issues relating to a student's behaviour/performance, these should have already been addressed previously, either via email, telephone call or – where necessary – a dedicated face-to-face meeting. Parents' evening simply isn't the time or the place for these kinds of potentially difficult conversations. They offer neither the private setting nor the time necessary to do justice to the type of delicate conversations that always have the potential to boil over and escalate. The time restrictions alone make this a no-go – not least if you're carrying out an online consultation and can see the clock quickly ticking down on your screen. So the simple message is: if you've got bad news to deliver, don't be tempted to wait until parents' evening. Grasp the initiative early and seek to control the variables.

Where parents' evening can be invaluable is in achieving three crucial aims:

Affirmation: one of the most empowering things you can do as a teacher is offer personalised praise to a student. When you get this right, it can be utterly transformative and the fact that you have identified a positive trait (perhaps something that the student concerned hadn't even been conscious of) can have the effect of hardwiring it into their future approach and making them keen to replicate the behaviours that have earned them praise in the first place. When you have the opportunity to relay this message in the presence of a parent it can be even more powerful.

Motivation: another of a teacher's most vital roles is to act as a coach and a motivator. Your job is to convince each of your students that they are capable of achieving things that they may initially believe are beyond their reach. You should be having face-to-face conversations like this on a daily basis. Often your efforts will be in vain and the student will return home still insisting to their parents 'I can't do it!' Parents' evening presents a golden opportunity to fix that. Suddenly you find yourself in the rare position where you can speak to the student while the other most influential adults in their life are also present and you have the opportunity to explain to all concerned that 'your child is far more capable than they give themselves credit for; if they work hard, they are more than capable of hitting their targets.' If handled correctly, the power of these conversations – with all key players present – cannot be overstated.

Clarification: this final aim is at least as important as the two which precede it but is arguably implemented less often and less effectively. How many times have you spent hours on end marking books and thinking to yourself 'I wonder if anyone actually reads my comments?' There's plenty of research out there which supports those doubts and the development of DIRT activities (Directed Improvement and Reflection Time) is an attempt to mitigate this. Parents' evenings also have a vital role to play though. What better opportunity are you going to have to go through the student's work, with both parent and child present, review targets, address any misunderstanding about these targets and even introduce the parents to ways in which they can support further progress at home? This, in many ways, is the most productive use of the limited time you have available at each parents' evening consultation.

Kids or no kids?

The biggest remaining question surrounding parents' evenings and the one that probably presents the biggest point of difference between schools is whether or not the students themselves should be present. As a new teacher, you're likely to have little control over this and will have to make the best of whichever scenario you're presented with. But, having experienced a range of formats and even having worked at a school where *Bingo!* (with the prospect of alcohol and nicotine as prizes) was introduced in order to encourage parental engagement, I'm happy to nail my own colours firmly to the mast.

The prospect of having a worthwhile consultation without the single most important individual being present is absurd.

This way of doing things was very much the norm during my school own days. I still have vivid memories of spending a frantic few days prior to each parents' evening putting on my best behaviour in the hope that this rearguard action would distract my teachers from my previous underperformance. I can also recall those torturous hours waiting for my mum to come home, wondering what the teachers had told her, and desperately trying to read her body language as she walked up the garden path at the end of the night. Invariably, her brief summation of the evening's interactions would go something along the lines of: 'Mr Carr and Mr Hunter both say you're doing OK but need to work harder, Mrs Howden says you talk too much in class, Mrs Webb still doesn't like you and Mr Preston says you're a "top lad".' And that would pretty much be that; no clear feedback on how to improve; no indication of future direction, let alone advice relating to careers or higher education. We'd just rinse and repeat the same process each year, with no real impact being made or any positive change being effected.

The prospect of having a worthwhile consultation without the single most important individual being present is absurd.

Thankfully, an increasing number of schools are waking up to the fact that bringing the students into the room and engaging them in the conversation makes the process far more worthwhile. It cements the home–school partnership, it (hopefully) signals to the student that their teacher and their parents are singing from the same hymn sheet and it also presents the opportunity to engage the parents in the learning process.

If your school is still one of those that chooses to exclude the students from the conversation and you find yourself in the position to influence change, I would strongly urge you to do so.

In the meantime, here are some final tips that should help you to make the most out of parents' evening, regardless of the format:

1. **Don't labour your points.** You're only likely to have five minutes at your disposal so use the time efficiently. Once you have made your point and parents/students have indicated that it's understood, move on.
2. **Ask, don't tell.** If you're fortunate enough to have the student present, try to avoid launching straight into a eulogy/diatribe and instead use this as an opportunity to assess how reflective/aware they are of their own application, attainment and progress. A simple question such as 'How do you think you're doing?' is an easy way to kickstart the conversation, ensure that the student is fully engaged with the process and provides a perfect opportunity for you to provide affirmation, motivation and clarification as part of your own response.
3. **Avoid comparisons with peers.** I still find it shocking that, even up to a few years ago, colleagues of mine would routinely rank the students in their class in school reports and then reinforce this negative message at parents' evenings. This should go completely against the grain for teachers nowadays and the message should always be

'You're competing to be the best version of yourself; your classmates' performance is irrelevant.' Unfortunately, some parents will still remember this as standard practice from their own school days and ask you questions like 'How are they doing compared to the rest of the class?' Make sure you bat away these questions and use this as an opportunity to politely *retrain* the parent concerned.

4. **Avoid making comparisons with siblings.** If you've been at a school for more than a year or two, you're almost certain to come across families where you have taught a couple of siblings – often with very contrasting experiences. While it's fine to ask about how the other child is getting on (it shows that you care and still have a genuine interest in their progress), never, ever be tempted to make comparisons between siblings. These stray comments are unfair, can be hugely damaging and may unlock resentment and insecurities that are already present.[1]

5. **Don't be afraid to be a human.** We talked earlier about the fact that some teachers feel more comfortable adopting a persona within the classroom and some will also feel the need to don the same mask at parents' evenings. Whether this is fuelled by insecurity or a desire to portray themselves as being professional, my advice is that you try to avoid this. More often than not, your idea of 'professional' will actually come across as cold and officious and place an unnecessary barrier between you and the parents. My advice (as long as this is something that comes naturally to you) is to be warm, seek to put the parents at ease and, above all else, convey the fact that you are all on the same team and share the same priority: achieving what's best for the student.

6. **Avoid jargon.** It's always worth remembering that (more often than not) the people sitting in front of you are not teachers, they aren't subject specialists and, if you choose to regale them with too much terminology or the minutiae of your exam board specification, they're not going to be impressed, they're going to be baffled. As parents, the chances are that the three most pressing questions they'll want

---

1. This may seem like a case of stating the obvious but I've lost count of the number of times where colleagues have got themselves in a mess by venturing down this road.

to be answered are: Is my child happy? Are they working hard? Are they doing well? Use these questions as your anchor point and then progress from there.

7. **Never talk down to parents.** This feels like another case of *stating the blindingly obvious* but, sadly, it still happens too often and I've even experienced it from the opposite side of the desk. Teaching is a great job, we work bloody hard and are rewarded with immense satisfaction, opportunities for career development and some generous (but extremely necessary) holiday entitlements. Despite this, holding a QTS certificate does not entitle the recipient to act like they are automatically the cleverest person in the room. Unfortunately, however, it still happens and a small minority of teachers still manage to give us all a bad name and, in the process, erect barriers that really aren't helpful. I've witnessed this first-hand when I've attended parents' evenings as a *civilian* at my children's schools. It still shocks me how many teachers habitually talk down to parents and, when asked perfectly reasonable questions, instinctively try to obfuscate behind a wall of jargon. In such situations, it's always fun to watch the reaction when you reveal that actually you're a teacher yourself. There's invariably a gulp, a blanching of the complexion and then, after a brief yet uncomfortable pause, you suddenly find yourself being addressed like an adult. Education is built on partnerships and you can only build these relationships effectively if they're based on equality and mutual respect.

CHAPTER 8:

Your role as a form tutor

It's true, being a form tutor can be a time-consuming (and often tiring) business. To start with, you'll have to be on hand to carry out the legal obligation of registering your tutees twice per day; you're also likely to be required to spend 20-30 minutes of 'form time' with your group and may have to devote energy to planning worthwhile activities in order to make productive use of this time. On top of this, you'll be expected to monitor the behaviour, application and progress of your tutees, instigating interventions where necessary; you'll be required to attend weekly tutor meetings; you'll have regular contact with parents to maintain, tutor comments to add to school reports and – just in case all of that was not quite enough – you'll also have to be on hand to provide encouragement and pick up the pieces whenever something goes wrong for one of the tutees who have been placed under your protective wing.

When you add all of this together and then load it on top of what's likely to be a full teaching timetable, the prospect can almost feel overwhelming and it's perhaps understandable why colleagues are occasionally keen to wriggle out of being a form tutor altogether. Stick with it though and your role as a form tutor can become one of the highlights of your job and can provide some much-needed moments of sunshine at those times when dark clouds are gathering elsewhere.

Being a form tutor can provide much-needed moments of sunshine at those times when dark clouds are gathering elsewhere.

The trick – as with most things in life – behind making the most of your time as a form tutor is to avoid half measures; if you're going to do something, go all out and commit to investing your whole self into doing as good a job as you can. If you're willing to make that leap, the rewards will be as profound for you as they are for your tutees and you'll be provided with daily reminders of why you've chosen a job that can be time-consuming, frustrating, exhausting and demoralising.

Making it work

A good form group should operate like a family. It can often feel like an eclectic mix of disparate individuals who at least appear to have been thrown together in haphazard fashion. It will take all of your skills as a teacher, diplomat and manager of people to somehow fuse sporty Alex, nerdy Mo, vacuous Ailsa, grumpy Jo and odd Jamie into a cohesive group but it can be a rewarding process. Often the most diverse selections of individuals can end up being the most cohesive groups and, if you follow these simple steps, everyone (including you) can benefit from these eclectic groupings:

1. **Establish and maintain high standards.** Form time should provide respite from formal lessons but that doesn't mean that you should adopt a casual approach. If your time together is going to be valuable you should set out and maintain the same high standards that ought to be in place for any other lesson. Although the focus may be different, you are still the teacher, they are still the students and the clear expectations should remain the same: they should arrive in a timely fashion; be correctly turned out; fully equipped; sit correctly behind their desks; engage fully in all activities and stick to all other regular expectations. I've seen form tutors misguidedly try to go for the *relaxed* approach and – worse – try to position themselves as a

friend rather than a teacher. As I stressed earlier, this approach doesn't work, it lowers standards and, ultimately, undermines the form tutor's authority. Your tutees will value a friendly, supportive relationship but what they actually want is an adult who can maintain boundaries, provide appropriate guidance and act as a role model. They have friends their own age.

2. **Establish regular home–school contact as soon as possible.** Schools that have a healthy focus on pastoral care will insist on this as a matter of policy but, regardless of the demands of your school, this is a valuable *minimum standard* that you'd be well advised to impose upon yourself. If your pastoral systems are working effectively, the form tutor should always be the first point of contact for parents. There may be issues that need escalating further up the chain of command but, in good times and in bad, the parents' first instinct should always be to reach out to the member of staff who they know and trust the most: the form tutor. Your job is to establish those relationships and build that trust. As a form tutor, you should start any academic year by contacting the parents of all of your tutees within the first week or so. Whether you choose to pick up the phone or send an email, the purpose is to introduce/reacquaint yourself, initiate dialogue and establish the important principles that:

   a. Your door is always open and parents should never hesitate to contact you.
   b. It's always better to flag up minor issues early, rather than allowing them to potentially develop into bigger problems.

3. **Make yourself accessible to your tutees.** If you're lucky, you'll be assigned to form time in your regular teaching room. If you're not, this process can be slightly more problematic. Either way, the principle remains that the best form tutors tend to be the ones who make themselves the most readily available throughout the day. You may have tutees who rush straight to you in times of crisis, you may have others who lack confidence and rely upon the reassuring presence of a permanent base, you may have some who appear to be largely indifferent and you may have others who will habitually gravitate to

your room for a chat (often at the most inconvenient times) or simply to ask you the most random questions ('Do French ducks "quack" in their own language, sir?'). Either way, your constant presence is an important anchor for these children and these interactions are the glue with which these relationships are bound together.

4. **Establish a 'team dynamic'.** We've already talked about establishing an identity and shared ethos within each of your teaching groups but this is even more critical when forging a cohesive form group. Whatever this identity ends up being needs to be an amalgam of your own values and the individual and collective characteristics of the group. Once enshrined, your group should operate as a *family*, with all members looking after one another – however disparate the individuals who comprise that unit may be. If you can master this delicate alchemy, there's every chance you'll be rewarded with some truly life-affirming moments and get to witness some hitherto unlikely friendships forming. This will all hinge upon your skill and commitment as a form tutor.

5. **Try to make your form room feel like** home. Even if you don't happen to be assigned to your regular teaching room, make sure that you're able to stamp your form's identity on the room – even if this simply involves commandeering a notice board or display. Your room (or at least the noticeboard) should be a reflection of the identity of the group you've worked hard to establish. There'll be generic stuff that you'll have to include (e.g. school rules, values, etc) but you should also use this to underline the culture and identity within your group and, wherever possible, involve the students in this process.

6. **Make productive use of your time.** Just as there are those who will adopt the casual approach to managing their form group, there are also those who will cling to the 'we just tend to chat' approach, as if this is a conscious decision rather than a tacit acknowledgment that the time they have with their form group isn't valuable. Some of the students will superficially embrace this *path of least resistance* because it's easy but, over time, the value of this daily contact time will be diminished, as will your authority as a form tutor and the relationship between you and your group. Form time can be fun, it can be relaxing but it has to be planned, structured and matched to the needs of

your group. In many schools, the approach to form time tends to be prescriptive, which can be both a blessing and a curse. On the one hand, it means that the onus of much of the planning is taken away from the form tutor, earning you back some much-needed time to attend to other competing priorities. On the other hand, it will limit your ability to shape a programme around the needs of your group. If you're fortunate, the school will provide a loose framework but also allow you sufficient latitude to adapt this programme around the needs of your form. Whatever the case, the important thing is that the time you have is structured, well-planned and effectively utilised.

Making the time count

Regardless of how prescriptive your school's approach to form time happens to be, there is a range of potential activities that can make it a really productive and positive part of the day. Some schools even take the decision to have PSHE delivered during form time and there's certainly some logic in assigning some of the most critical and sensitive lessons to the person who should – in theory – know the students best.

There are various other activities that could be used to make productive use of the time; the key, as always, is in ensuring that they are adapted in order to meet the needs and identity of your group:

1. **'Housekeeping.'** OK, so not the most inspiring idea to kick things off but, in many ways, the most essential. In the morning, during that frantic five minutes or so when you meet your legal obligation of registering the group, you need to find the time to check on their wellbeing (the better you get to know them as individuals, the more intuitively you will be able to read the signs), relay any important messages and also check that your troops are dressed and ready to go out to battle. As form tutors, you really are the first bastions of defence when it comes to maintaining standards within the school. So take the time to check uniform and equipment, stress the importance of good time keeping and – where possible – ensure that each individual is in the right frame of mind to have a successful day. If this

sounds like a tall order, the bad news is that you'll have to repeat the whole process when the students return frazzled, dishevelled and windswept[2] at the end of lunch. With this in mind, it's always worth dedicating one of your 20-30 minute form time sessions each week to 'housekeeping' in order to provide you with additional time to check on all these essentials, along with other key matters such as totting up merits, signing planners, etc.

2. **Quizzes.** Sometimes the simplest ideas are the best and, if you want something that provides engagement, expands/rewards knowledge and introduces a dose of healthy competition, you really can't go wrong with quizzes. There are literally millions of off-the-peg quizzes that are ready and waiting to be used online but, if you do have the time and the inclination, quizzes that are bespoke to your group tend to work best. Quizzes can be a great way of supporting revision of the wider curriculum (particularly if you're able to collaborate with like-minded colleagues), improving general knowledge and helping the students to take an interest in the wider world – something that has never been more important than it is right now. The important thing is that quizzes are suitably challenging, avoid simply pandering to the lowest common denominator ('Who was voted off *Love Island* last night?') and are inclusive, with any competition being friendly rather than oppressive or demeaning. Simple tweaks like arranging your tutees into strategically chosen groups and pairs will help but much will ultimately come down to how successfully you've introduced a positive, supportive culture to your form already.

3. **Mindfulness/mental wellbeing activities.** We'll look at mental health and its impact in a little more detail later on but form time presents a perfect platform to support your tutees' wellbeing and even introduce some mindfulness activities. Some schools will already mandate that at least one session per week is reserved for this purpose but, whether or not your school determines this as part of a prescribed programme, there is a whole smorgasbord of options available to you. This could range from taking part in mindfulness activities, watching

---

2. When I first started teaching, I was told by a senior colleague that 'windy lunchtimes are terrible because it does something to their brains' but I swiftly dismissed it as an old wives' tale. It turns out it's 100% true though: wind + kids = carnage!

and discussing one of the growing number of useful videos and talks that are available online or simply providing the opportunity to discuss experiences in a structured, controlled and supportive setting. The important thing, as always, is that the students themselves are allowed at least some input into what this time involves and that you take the time to periodically assess the impact and worthwhileness of your chosen activities. Whatever programme you come up with between you though, this really is precious time.

4. **Current affairs.** When you have kids of your own (assuming you haven't already), I'm certain you'll take the time to ensure that they are fully engaged with the world around them, understand the impact that politics can have on their day-to-day lives and can articulate their thoughts on these topics confidently. When you speak to your students though – regardless of the school setting – there's every chance you'll be shocked at how few households provide these valuable formative experiences for their children and how few families even buy a newspaper regularly. Whether it's because they fail to see the benefit of investing this time or they simply don't have the time to invest, many parents aren't having these vital conversations with their kids – and that's where you come in. Simply designating a day each week where you can read and discuss current affairs from a newspaper (teacher hack: if you travel to work via public transport, you can 'liberate' a few copies of the *Metro* and put them to good civic use) or watching a news report online, can provide the opportunity to broaden the students' horizons and trigger valuable discussions.

5. **Class discussions.** Once you've fired the students' enthusiasm for current affairs and inspired them to take a more active interest in the world around them, what better way to build on that than through a class discussion? The trick here is to ensure that any discussion is structured, inclusive and respectful (rather than a free-for-all that'll tend to be dominated by the loudest voices). Your English department should be able to provide you with resources or ideas for activities but my advice would be to choose defined topics and then supply each student with 'action cards', featuring words like *support, challenge, develop*, etc, in order to ensure that everybody takes part and the more vocal students don't drown out their more reserved peers.

6. **Reading.** If you're reading this book, there's every chance that you're either a teacher already or in the process of training to be a teacher, so I won't need to emphasise the importance of literacy across the curriculum and why we should grasp every opportunity to establish reading a book, in silence, without distractions, as an absolutely indispensable life habit. Most studies conclude that children ought to read for a minimum of 20 minutes per day and, coincidentally, that's around the time most form periods last, so why not put this time to good use? Whether the students are responsible for providing their own reading material (with the teacher ensuring that it is appropriate) or you choose to read aloud to the class (there are plenty of studies that attest to the power of this approach), this can be a really valuable use of everybody's time – including yours. Make sure that you don't neglect your own responsibility to model good behaviour though: it may be tempting to use this period of tranquillity to catch up with paperwork or mark a few exercise books but it'll be a more powerful statement if you practice what you preach, so treat yourself to 20 minutes of reading for pleasure too.

7. **Projects/activism.** Young people are often (wrongly) accused of apathy so, if they feel passionate about an issue, form time is the perfect opportunity to guide and encourage them to channel this enthusiasm in a positive manner. Whether it's researching a topic or issue that they feel strongly about or even writing a formal letter to their local MP, if you're able to focus this passion it's a really valuable use of this time.

8. **Create a kindness wall.** This is a brilliant idea that I've stolen shamelessly from a former colleague but it really does work a treat. Basically, you create a noticeboard where students get to anonymously display kind/complimentary comments about their peers ('Joe always cheers me up when he comes to form as he has a great sense of humour and always has something funny to say'). My particularly talented and creative colleague created her kindness wall in the form of a tree, with each student able to attach leaves featuring complimentary comments and anecdotes but, whatever it looks like, the key thing is that you are taking the opportunity to underscore a culture of support and kindness.

Mentoring

Of all of the support measures and interventions you will be expected to put in place as a form tutor, mentoring can be one of the most powerful. Thankfully, an increasing number of schools are putting structures in place that set aside time for form tutors to carry out coaching/mentoring with their tutees on a consistent and regular basis. But whether you are fortunate enough to work at a school that prioritises mentoring in this manner or you are forced to carve out the time at break/lunch yourself, it's important that you make this time count.

One slightly odd development within some schools is for mentoring to be artificially demarcated as either 'pastoral' or 'academic' as if the two areas are mutually exclusive. They clearly aren't and, more often than not, a student's academic progress will be predicated (or at least strongly influenced) by their overall sense of wellbeing. With that in mind, the first simple (yet fundamental) question of any coaching/mentoring session should almost always be 'How are you feeling?'

On a day-to-day basis, this question can often be reduced to little more than a phatic utterance or a conversation starter to fill awkward silences ('How are you?'...'Fine, how about you?'). Yet, in this context, it can mean so much more and can offer the invitation for a young person to share their inner-most fears and feelings with a trusted adult. If nothing else, it underlines the important message that they are supported and surrounded by people who care.

The first simple (yet fundamental) question of any coaching/mentoring session should always be 'How are you feeling?'

This question is far more than an opening gambit and it's essential that once you have opened this particular door, you take the time to listen. For many students, the response may well be 'Fine thanks' but for others you may prompt them to open up about an issue that has been bottled up and inhibiting them for some time. Your role in this situation is not to provide answers but simply to listen in the first instance. Should the student's disclosure raise any potential safeguarding concerns, you are bound by due process and need to be open about this. But if they don't, it's advisable to let the student feel that they are in control of the situation while offering support and empathy. Simple questions like 'What do you want to happen?' or 'Is there anything I can do to help?' signal your support while allowing the child to feel that they still maintain an element of control. As tempting as it may be to leap straight into *intervention mode*, doing so without the child's endorsement may make them less likely to open up about future issues, for fear of setting a chain of events in motion which they feel they have little control over.

If intervention is required, this will often involve communicating with parents, colleagues or even peers. In each instance, tact and diplomacy are essential as there is always a risk that you could inadvertently make things worse or – if nothing else – make the student more reluctant to speak out in future.

> *'What do you think you could do differently?'*
> *is always a much more positive starting point*
> *than 'You need to stop doing this!'*

Where direct intervention is not required, it's always good practice to avoid leaping in with prescriptive solutions and instead to employ more careful questioning in order to encourage reflection and (hopefully) guide the student to solutions of their own. 'What do you think you could do differently?' is always a much more positive starting point than 'You need to stop doing this!'

On those occasions where your mentoring session needs to be steered towards issues of academic performance and attainment, it's absolutely essential that you stick doggedly to the mantra of focusing on processes rather than outcomes, reinforce the message that the only person they are in competition with is themselves and – again – use questioning as a means of leading the student to their own conclusions (and ultimately their own solutions).

Though it may be tempting for you to lead with the data that you have been furnished with (e.g. 'I can see you're not doing too well in maths'), it's likely to be far more productive to try to find out how self-aware they are of their own performance. As such, asking questions like 'Which subjects are going well at the moment?' and then digging deeper with follow up questions like 'Why do you think you're able to perform well in that subject?' is likely to lead to more positive, student-led outcomes. You can then call upon the data in order to provide affirmation ('I can see you're doing well in maths because your test scores are great') or – where necessary – to probe further around discrepancies between the student's perception and the teachers' assessment. Again though, sensitivity is paramount: the data you have at your disposal can be an incredibly powerful tool but – if utilised as a blunt instrument – it can be damaging and demoralising.

Ultimately, the most important data is that relating to the students' effort and application. Even if the attainment isn't quite where it needs to be, it's the student's willingness to work hard that has to be your focus and it's the job of the form tutor to encourage the student to keep doing the right thing – even if gratification has to be deferred ('Keep working hard and persevering, and the results will come'). Where there is a disparity between attitude, application and attainment, there's also the opportunity to probe for diagnostic issues and, where necessary, liaise with colleagues.

It's not uncommon in some schools for the format of mentoring to be fairly prescriptive and to hinge upon a set of pre-written questions or even the generation of quantitative data. If this is the case, it's important that you follow whatever procedures have been set out for you consistently but it's also essential that you use your own judgement, focus on the individual sitting in front of you and lead off with that all-important opening question that we talked about earlier. Mentoring should never be a box-ticking exercise and, the minute it begins looking like it is, its value is immediately diminished.

Report writing

One area where you are almost certain to be called into action as a form tutor is to add comments to school reports. With a growing number of schools eschewing any kind of qualitative information in reports and relying instead on raw data, your ability to provide colour and an all-important personal touch is even more imperative.

While it is essential that you have a thorough understanding of the picture that the data paints and are able to summarise effectively, it is essential that your comments aren't simply a dry rehash. Instead, your comments need to be a far more personal appraisal of the whole person, taking into account what they bring to the school, how they are performing in their lessons and what they need to do in order to progress. This is, of course, more challenging when the student is neither performing to expectations nor making a particularly positive contribution to the school. But it is on these occasions where your understanding of your audience and your sensitivity to the power of your words becomes ever more critical.

> *It is essential that your comments aren't simply a dry rehash of the data.*

Too often, however, form tutor comments can be somewhat perfunctory, demonstrating little understanding or value of the individual. For example: 'Jade is a popular member of the form who usually arrives on time to registration. She is performing well in maths, English and science but needs to work harder in food technology, religious studies and history. She is a member of the school netball team and attends weekly training sessions.'

All of this information may well be accurate but, from a parent's perspective, it provides little indication that the member of staff who supposedly has the closest relationship with their child actually knows or values them as an individual. Moreover, the information provided is little more than a soulless retread of the data already supplied.

However, with a little more care, attention and the ability to draw upon meaningful relationships (including effective mentoring), the same information can be presented in a far more positive and compelling manner: 'Jade is a highly regarded member of the group whose warmth and humour brighten up form time. She plays an active role in the life of the school and is a valuable and committed member of the school netball team. This is an encouraging report, with several areas where Jade is matching and even surpassing her targets. However, there are still some areas where Jade needs to seek improvement and where she herself has acknowledged the need to focus more during lessons and devote more time to study outside of class. Nevertheless, I am confident that, with her positive outlook and a little more consistency, Jade is more than capable of making these adjustments.'

A few carefully chosen words can make a world of difference.

Vertical or horizontal?

The most significant factor that will impact the manner in which you manage your form group is likely to be something that is beyond your control: the make-up of the group. We've already talked about the importance of defining the identity of your group and enshrining a shared ethos that is relevant to them but there are also other key variables which need to be considered.

Most schools still employ fairly traditional *horizontal* tutoring systems, with students grouped with peers from their own year groups. Less conventional *vertical* form groups are used elsewhere, however, and there are pros and cons attached to each of these systems.

Horizontal form groups are, in many respects, a much more straight-forward proposition. With all of the students being the same age, it's easier to plan relevant activities for form time and, assuming the school concerned doesn't have an unhealthy tendency to tinker, the form tutor has the opportunity to build effective relationships with the students and their families and to provide continuity from Year 7 all the way to the end of Year 11 (and sometimes beyond). Pastoral leadership within this kind of set-up is also more easily implemented, with a head of year usually responsible for the progress and behaviour of each individual year group.

On face value, vertical groups can be more problematic but, if a positive culture has already been established, they can deliver a number of benefits.

On face value, vertical groups can be more problematic. Planning appropriate activities can be more challenging when catering for an age range that can span age 11-16 (and occasionally 11-18) and, although in theory the older students should act as mentors/role models, their influence may not always be positive or desirable – particularly in those schools which are in the early stages of instigating cultural change.

Nonetheless, if a positive culture has already been established, vertical tutoring can deliver a number of significant benefits and any drawbacks can be mitigated by opting for a *halfway house* whereby the groups are vertical in each key stage (so form groups made up of Years 7-9, 10-11, 12-13).

Those schools that opt for vertical forms tend to also base their pastoral structures around a 'house' system. People may immediately associate this with traditional inter-house competition, conjuring up images of *Tom Brown's School Days* and even *Harry Potter* but, from a pastoral perspective, this can also yield numerous benefits. Placing siblings within the same house, as part of a vertical tutoring system, can mean that parents can establish long-lasting relationships with key individuals (such as the form tutor and head of house) who are already familiar with them and their family history – including any potential issues. Alongside other older students within the vertical forms, siblings can provide support and guidance to the younger students within their groups, with the mix of ages creating a family dynamic of its own.

Whichever system your school happens to opt for, however, the fundamentals remain the same: get to know the students within your group; build strong home–school partnerships; be accessible; make valuable use of form time. If you can do this, everyone – including you – will benefit.

Coping with the other 'added extras'

If you've read all this and are already wondering 'How am I going to cope?' be warned, we're not finished yet! As well as being a (hopefully) outstanding teacher, writing reports, attending parents' evenings and being a constant source of guidance and support in your role as a form tutor, there are a couple of other *added extras* that you will need to factor into your working week...

On duty!

First up, in most schools you will be expected to be part of a duty team, with a focus on supervising the students at break, lunch and sometimes before and after school. This might involve a day each week where you'll be assigned multiple duties or a number of duties spread across the course of the week. If you're fortunate, the kind soul compiling the rota may take your teaching load into account before assigning duties but, from my experience, you're just as likely to find that basic necessities like eating your lunch or popping to the loo begin to feel like luxuries. Unfortunately, like death and taxes, duties are pretty much unavoidable; it's just a matter of making the most of the time you've been assigned.

Your experience as a member of the duty team can vary drastically from school to school. I've worked in schools where lunch duty on the yard could be reminiscent of a prison movie, with the *inmates* hemmed in, projectiles flying overhead and a constant sense of menace always hanging in the air. Elsewhere, both the surroundings and prevailing mood can make lunch duty a far more tranquil experience – to the point when even staff who aren't on the rota will voluntarily pop out to lend a hand. Whatever the scenario you happen to be faced with, there are a number of things you can do to make the time more worthwhile – even if you don't end up getting fed!

1. **Use this as an opportunity to build relationships.** There will always be certain students who, as hard as you may try, you will struggle to build strong relationships with as a classroom teacher. The fact that your modus operandi is to teach chemistry and they *hate* chemistry can, quite naturally, present something of a barrier. Outside of your lab/classroom, there's the perfect opportunity to get to know students in a different setting – without the added pressure of occasionally having to force square pegs through round holes. You can use your time on duty to reframe your relationships with some students and the time you invest out on the yard can often pay dividends back in the classroom.

2. **Act as an early warning system.** As a member of the duty team, you have a potentially crucial role to play in keeping the children safe. In the first instance, your ability to keep your eyes and ears open can be the difference between a schoolyard accident happening or not happening, can prevent a fight breaking out and can enable you to intervene in the face of the merest hint of bullying. On a wider level, your vigilance can be even more important.

   When provided with the camouflage of a classroom, alongside 30 other students, unhappy children are incredibly adept at blending in and going unnoticed. In the expanse of a school yard, these unhappy children often stand out a mile. Your vigilance and proactiveness can result in these children being identified and supported much more quickly than may otherwise have been the case. Similarly, if you are stationed at the dining hall serving area, you might well have your hands full keeping the Year 11 boys in check but you'll also be perfectly placed to see which children are skipping lunch and which others are surreptitiously scraping what little food they have straight into the bin. Your role here might seem like a weighty appendage on top of an already busy day but your presence is priceless.

3. **Make a positive difference.** As tempting as it may be to gain some respite from another busy day and perhaps even catch up with colleagues, you can probably see by now the importance of having your eyes and ears open around school – particularly when you are on duty. Your vigilance will indeed keep children safe but, beyond that, it can also help to make them happy. So don't just look out for

the potential accident or the brewing scuffle; keep an eye out for the awkward lonely kid in the corner or the quiet student sitting alone in the canteen. You may be tired and emotionally drained and there's no doubt you deserve *five minutes to yourself* but those same five minutes may well make a world of difference to an unhappy child. There's a small chance they may take the opportunity to open up about a problem they're experiencing but they're just as likely to want to regale you with the minutiae of *Minecraft*, TikTok or any number of niche topics or interests. They might even (ever-so-politely) make it clear that they don't actually want to talk with you at all (being spotted chatting to a teacher is seldom seen as *cool!*). The thing that matters is that you've made the most of the time available and given some attention to a child who might often feel invisible.

In these situations, however stressed and busy I may be, my cue is always: *what if that was my child*? Once you view things through that lens – regardless of whether you do have kids of your own – it's easy to do the right thing.

Extracurricular clubs and activities

If you read certain sections of the press or choose to listen to certain politicians, you could be excused for thinking that not only do we teachers have an abundance of time on our hands but we also have the capacity to cure many of the world's ills. *Lengthen the school day? No problem! Shorten the holidays? You betcha! Cure the obesity crisis? Sign me up now!*

The truth is, even without all of these added extras, most of us are just about managing to keep our heads above water. Without labouring the death and taxes analogy, the chances are that we will also be compelled to find time to run an extracurricular activity and we're again faced with the choice of whether to embrace this or treat it as a beast of burden.

Now I can empathise with those teachers who choose the latter path and I've even worked with colleagues who have come up with spectacularly unappealing clubs and activities in the hope that no children would turn up (Sudoku Club anyone?). Invariably however, like Bialystock and Bloom in Mel Brooks' *The Producers*, those guaranteed flops can occasionally turn into unexpected hits. My advice therefore is to go for it and apply much of the same logic as you would to your break/lunch duty.

Your attempts to 'make geography fun!' may well be lost on the Year 10 boys but they'll see you in an entirely different light when you're knee deep in mud and coaching rugby on a dark Tuesday afternoon. Equally, building model aeroplanes or hunting Pokémon may not be your thing but it could be the highlight of some children's weeks and could open doors to friendship for some of the most vulnerable students in your school.

Teaching can either be a backbreaking and demoralising job that places impossible demands on those daft enough to sign up for it, or it can be a rewarding vocation that always compels you to *go the extra mile*. Try to choose the latter path.

CHAPTER 9:

Keeping your students safe

One or two teachers out there still labour under the misconception that their number one priority is to ensure that the students they teach perform as well as possible in their subject. These teachers are wrong and, what's more, the law makes it quite clear that they're wrong. The single most important obligation we have – both as individuals and institutionally – is to keep children safe. Anything else is a very distant second behind that single core purpose.

Amanda Spielman, who at the time of writing is Ofsted's chief inspector, caused consternation in education circles when she appeared to accuse some schools of prioritising student wellbeing over academic performance during the lockdown of 2020. She claimed that 'In a lot of schools it felt as though their attention went very rapidly to the most disadvantaged children, into making food parcels, going out visiting.

'They put a great deal of attention into the children with greatest difficulties, which is admirable, but in some cases that probably got prioritised.'[3]

Her comments appeared to make an implied criticism when comparing state schools to their counterparts in the independent sector. Unfortunately, she seemed to overlook the fact that for many independent schools maintaining

---

3.   The Independent. (2021) *Ofsted chief says schools may have prioritised food parcels over education in lockdown.* Available at: https://www.independent.co.uk/news/education/education-news/ofsted-food-parcels-covid-lockdown-b1919884.html#r3z-addoor (Accessed: 24 September 2021).

an expected level of service for fee-paying parents was a financial imperative and few, if any, would have had to concern themselves unduly over whether the students in their care were likely to have been fed. More critically, however passionate we are about pedagogy and how dedicated we are to achieving the best possible educational outcomes, all of this pales into insignificance when placed against the importance of ensuring that these same children are being fed and cared for. Ultimately, you don't need to consult Maslow's hierarchy of needs in order to determine that putting food in hungry young bellies during a global crisis probably trumps the importance of making sure there's a maths test on Google Classroom by 9am. If you do find yourself wavering on that judgement, you perhaps need to adjust your moral compass or possibly consider an alternative career as a traffic warden.

Whatever other competing priorities you may be faced with, safeguarding has to take precedence over everything. And here's the thing: if children aren't happy and safe they're unlikely to perform anyway and, even if they do, those achievements count for little if they aren't in a position to enjoy them.

Without doubt the most difficult experience of my teaching career was receiving a message via social media informing me that a student I'd taught (and had done my best to support during some difficult times) at a previous school seven years earlier had died by suicide at the age of 23. Inevitably, as well as tears and frustration, this prompted me to question whether I, as a subject teacher, or we, as a school, had done enough to support that scared, bewildered but absolutely incredible young person back when they were 15 years old, with a whole world of possibilities ahead of them.

I'll never know the answer to that question but one thing it did bring clearly into focus was the fact that I would do everything I possibly could to ensure that no other young person I worked with would feel so despairing of life that they would feel compelled to erase any chance of a happy future.

The sad fact is that, although we live in times of comparative comfort and privilege, our children face more threats to their wellbeing (both from external factors and from issues locked inside their own minds) than ever before. As teachers, whether we were drawn to the profession through a love of subject or a passion for pedagogy, our overwhelming priority has to be to act as a first line of defence – and it's a job that we can't afford to get wrong.

Safeguarding

Every school in the UK is obliged by law to appoint a Designated Safeguarding Lead (DSL). In some schools there will only be one DSL, in others the role may be shared, and in all schools there needs to be a clear contingency in place if the DSL is absent for any reason.

If you happen to find yourself working in a school where you don't actually know who the DSL is, it signals two things: firstly, a clear failing on the part of the school – by the very nature of their role, the DSL needs to be prominent, visible and accessible to all members of your school community; and secondly, before you do anything else, you need to find out who that person is and ensure that you have a thorough understanding of your school's safeguarding procedures.

Safeguarding issues have a tendency to land at your door when you least expect them and you need to be ready to handle them flawlessly, without missing a beat. A child's wellbeing (or even their life) may depend on your competency. That may sound overwhelming but it's a responsibility that you signed up for the second you accepted the king's shilling, and it's an obligation we always need to be ready and able to fulfil.

> *Whatever other competing priorities you may be faced with, safeguarding has to take precedence over everything.*

Safeguarding is, in many ways, a many-headed Hydra as well as a shape-shifting beast. Just as quickly as you can find solutions to old problems, new unheard-of problems can emerge, while the older issues adapt and change shape but never stop being a threat. Every year the government publishes its 'Keeping Children Safe in Education' (KCSIE) guidelines and every year a new set of issues and challenges will be brought under the spotlight. You may feel that you have a good handle on safeguarding but each year a new threat will emerge (FGM, County Lines, peer-on-peer abuse – the list keeps growing and it won't stop) and you will have to familiarise yourself not only with new terminology but also with the tell-tale signs of a growing number of threats. The one fatal error you can make in these situations is to think to yourself 'That couldn't happen here.' It most certainly could and it might already be occurring; any hint of complacency could be potentially fatal.

As a bare minimum, your school should provide updated safeguarding training for all staff at least once a year, with a focus on ensuring that they understand both the school's procedures and the content of the latest KCSIE document. New staff should also be inducted and briefed thoroughly on arrival (if you arrive at a new school and this doesn't happen, don't be afraid to ask why it hasn't). Ideally, however, safeguarding training should happen all the time and should be a fixed item on every agenda within the school. Inspecting bodies such as Ofsted will ensure that your school is compliant (and safeguarding is one area where there is no room for benefit of the doubt). Regardless of your school's confidence and clarity, there are a number of things that you can do yourself in order to maintain your own professional and moral obligations:

1. **Arm yourself with knowledge.** Every teacher should have a thorough understanding of their safeguarding responsibilities and a sound knowledge of the contents of the latest KCSIE document; every school should support that development of knowledge and should ensure that their safeguarding procedures are clear and well understood by all staff. If you are unfortunate enough to find yourself in a school that is not watertight in terms of its safeguarding obligations, make it your business to do all that you can to ensure that your knowledge and understanding is up-to-date and secure. Safeguarding concerns can arise when you least expect them and your ability to respond to them appropriately really can be a matter of life and death.

1. **Always err on the side of caution.** Often when you see or hear something untoward your instinct will tell you immediately that this is a potential safeguarding issue and you'll refer it to your DSL without hesitation. There will be other occasions, however, when you are not so sure and may suspect there to be a more benign explanation of what's going on. My rule of thumb in these situations is simple: it's far better to overreact than to under-react. Play it safe; speak to your DSL.

2. **Never assume it's already being dealt with.** There'll be other occasions where an issue arises but you're pretty sure that the DSL is already on the case. Never assume. Follow the procedures; make the referral. Even if other colleagues have already done so, you are removing any chance of a serious issue slipping through the cracks, while also providing your DSL with a broader range of evidence to investigate.

3. **Gather information.** If a child chooses you as the person they wish to make a disclosure to, you've been placed in a position of great responsibility and trust. Your natural inclination in such a situation may be to hightail straight to your DSL but, before you do so, pause for a moment. Children rarely make disclosures freely; this particular child has chosen this particular moment to open up to *you*, so make sure you listen and gather as much information as you can while they feel safe and lucid. Avoid asking any leading questions, make note of verbatim comments when it's appropriate to do so but, in the meantime, listen. Your job is not to decide whether this is a serious issue or to reach any kind of conclusion; your job is to gather information and support the child. Once you are confident that you have fulfilled both objectives, head straight to your DSL.

4. **Be discreet and confidential.** If a colleague or friend chose to share some sensitive, personal information with you, your first impulse wouldn't be rush to the staffroom and discuss this *gossip* with your workmates. When a child makes a disclosure, your approach should be no different. Although you have a legal responsibility – not to mention a moral obligation – to follow procedures and report any potential concerns to your DSL, it's always worth remembering that children have just as much right to privacy as adults do. If that right to privacy isn't respected, it may just present a barrier to future disclosures being made.

5. **Don't expect to receive an outcome.** It's tempting to think that once you've made a referral to your DSL that you'll be entitled to an update on the situation and – better still – some kind of resolution. Unfortunately, that simply isn't the case. Your referral may just represent one fragment of a patchwork of information that your DSL is working with and there may well be valid reasons (including the child's right to privacy) why they cannot provide you with any update or further information. The staff responsible for safeguarding within your school will often have to make sensitive and complex decisions about which information to share and which other information to withhold. Once you've fulfilled your own professional responsibilities, you need to trust them to do their job.

6. **Avoid the 'messiah complex'.** When a child chooses you as the recipient of a disclosure, you may well experience a flush of responsibility and a sense that it's your job to fix things. The fact that you've chosen to enter a caring profession makes this reaction wholly understandable but it's essential that you do maintain a level of professional detachment, both for the sake of the young person and yourself. Focus on providing support and empathy at the point of contact and then follow your safeguarding procedures to the letter but, from there, trust your colleagues and don't allow yourself to be crippled by an overwhelming sense of responsibility.

7. **Look after yourself.** Many disclosures are likely to expose you to upsetting information and, being an empathetic person, it's likely that hearing this will have a significant impact on you too. Colleagues who work in pastoral care will often talk about being *sponges* for all of the distressing things they see or hear over the course of a working day. It's vital that you are able to *empty the sponge* and can offload to a colleague (if you take it home it can impact on your own mental health). Just be sure to choose the most appropriate colleague in order to avoid breaching confidentiality (your DSL/pastoral team are likely to be accustomed to supporting colleagues almost as much as the students).

As far as safeguarding is concerned, your eyes and ears are essential. They'll allow you to spot the more obvious physical signs of self-harm or neglect but, over time, you'll also become more attuned to some of the less noticeable warnings and even subtle changes of mood, routine or demeanour that may highlight a potential problem. As a caring and approachable teacher, you're also more likely to be the adult a child will trust to make a potentially life-changing disclosure to and, as we've already made abundantly clear, you need to be ready to respond in that moment. The quality of your relationships will also never be more important than they are when it comes to safeguarding. The stronger these bonds are, the more likely it is that you may be alerted by another student or even a parent towards a potential issue that you may have been hitherto unaware of. The key is to be ready to respond.

Bullying

Of all the threats to children's wellbeing that lurk among us, bullying is arguably the most stubborn and adaptable. Bullying may not look the same as it once did and it may be harder to spot but it does just as much damage as it always has done.

If (like me) you're a child of the 1980s, your experience of bullying was probably that of something that was overt, physical (or at least openly verbal) and too often ignored by teachers. Times have, thankfully, changed. Schools have a legal obligation to tackle bullying and, as a society, it's an issue that we're collectively eager to call out. Unfortunately, in the face of increasingly robust resistance, bullying has changed too and, in many ways, has become more insidious. Our response to a more subtle and cunning enemy has to be to become even more alert.

Although it may be less prevalent, physical bullying still happens every day and, although it may masquerade beneath the veneer of 'we're only messing around – we're friends!' it needs to be stamped on (metaphorically at least). Name calling or – to give it a more accurate label – verbal bullying must also be met with *zero tolerance*. The dreaded B word ('It was only banter!') cannot be used as cover for the kind of persistent nastiness that blights young lives and can often burrow deep into the psyche of damaged adults. We must neither accept nor encourage 'banter' in our classrooms or our corridors.

As damaging as these twin evils are though, those children affected could once at least seek refuge in the relative safety of their own homes. Bullying circa the 21st century knows no such boundaries. The arrival of social media has, of course, shifted the paradigm. As a result, nowhere is safe. Even in the supposed haven of your own bedroom, the ominous *ping* of a mobile phone can open the door to vitriol and pain that can inflict both immediate and lasting damage. The frustration for us teachers is that something that we have little – if any – control over can render a seismic impact in our classrooms. Nonetheless, when this perfidious form of bullying rears its head – and inevitably leaves a footprint – we need to be ready to respond just as robustly and promptly as we would when a punch has been thrown or a slur has been hissed across a classroom.

At the risk of sounding like a stuck record, the strength of the relationships that you've built will be critical here. If you've put the groundwork into relationship building, the chances are that students are more likely to come forward to make disclosures about cyberbullying that either they or others are being subjected to. It's not unusual for parents to come forward after being alerted to this issue either, if they feel that you are trustworthy, will act with discretion (often to keep their own children out of the firing line) and will respond swiftly and effectively.

Although it can go undetected for long periods, the one saving grace where cyberbullying is concerned is that – through screen grabs – it's very easy to prove and, assuming your school has its policies in order, should also be relatively easily squashed.

There's also a significant educational angle that cannot be overlooked. Different schools will have drastically contrasting attitudes to the presence of mobile technology in the classroom. Some will be liberal, others will be prohibitive and some will even embrace the use of mobile technology as an intrinsic part of the learning experience. Whatever your school's approach, it's important that your students are encouraged to develop empathy and have an appreciation of the searing impact a few hastily typed words can have. It's also essential that they are fully cognisant of the potential legal implications of their actions; cyberbullying isn't just hurtful and morally wrong, it's potentially criminal behaviour and can be dealt with accordingly.

The school's educational responsibility does not stop there, however. Parents too must understand the impact (and implications) of their children's actions and must be encouraged to take as much responsibility for their behaviour online as their physical actions offline; ignorance cannot be an acceptable form of defence. The fact that cyberbullying invariably leaves a trail of concrete evidence means that even those parents with a tendency to defend the indefensible can be brought into line pretty quickly. Often the things that children are capable of typing behind the relative anonymity of a screen are shocking and tend to be things that they would not dream of saying out loud in the 'real world'. This cognitive dissonance is hugely problematic but, when faced with it through the sharing of a few well-chosen verbatim comments, can often prompt parents to take a little more interest (and responsibility) in their children's online activity. This doesn't fix the problem altogether but it's a start.

Wherever it occurs (and that unfortunately does occasionally include the staffroom), we need to be vigilant in the face of all forms of bullying and resolute in our response.

Mental health

Like bullying, mental health is a clear and present threat to our children's wellbeing which refuses to sit still and is able to evolve much more quickly than we are able to adapt to existing problems. Schools are waking up to the so-called 'mental health epidemic' but, while a growing number are keen to talk about what was previously a taboo topic, too much of this discussion is framed around empty platitudes ('It's OK not to be OK!' or 'It's good to talk!') and too few schools are able to back this up with concrete and effective action.

The sad truth is that, while we're ready to talk about mental health now, we're still woefully ill-equipped to deal with it. And that lack of resource and expertise is no more worryingly apparent than it is in our schools.

We teachers may be 'Jacks of all trades' but, with the best will in the world and even with an encouraging increase in the amount of online training now available, we do not have the time or capacity to become fully-fledged mental health professionals. What's worse is that – to our nation's great shame – there are not enough of those mental health professionals out there to meet the needs of our most vulnerable young people. Organisations such as CAMHS (the Child and Adolescent Mental Health Services) are completely swamped, the range of other services out there is not always easily navigable by schools, parents or youngsters, and government funding remains pitifully inadequate. To paraphrase the immortal line from *Jaws*, 'We really are going to need a bigger boat!'

In the meantime, much of the heavy lifting is going to fall onto the shoulders of – you guessed it! – the teaching profession. If we're going to cope with the strain and meet the increasing needs of our students, we're going to have to stick to many of the mantras outlined throughout this book: our availability to listen, our determination to build positive relationships and our willingness to give up our time (and our full attention).

The fact remains, however, that no matter how diligently we pursue these aims, we are not experts and, when presented with mental health issues by students, parents or colleagues, our ultimate response should always be to direct them to the professionals (starting with the GP) so that they can benefit from the most appropriate intervention. Nevertheless, it doesn't hurt to be well informed. There is some really good guidance out there – including a range of Mental Health First Aid training geared specifically towards those working in education. In addition, despite the growing number of conditions and manifestations that are out there, it's also worth being able to recognise the three 'old enemies' that often lie at the core of other issues:

1. **Stress.** This is probably the most commonly found of the 'big three' mental health issues and can often provide the gateway to its two bigger and more insidious siblings. In its initial manifestation, stress is a perfectly natural response to external stimuli and can even be a positive thing, invoking a 'fight or flight' response that brings the

optimum performance out of the individual concerned. Unfortunately, that's not always the case and, although the pressure of a big game can unlock greatness in certain individuals, the stress of the same situation can completely consume others and lead to even bigger problems. The main trigger for stress is where the demands of a situation exceed an individual's capability (or at least their perceived capability). We teachers need to be acutely aware of this. While it is perfectly acceptable (and, indeed, desirable) to present our students with challenging tasks, it's essential that they are pitched at a level that is appropriate for the individual. Moreover, each challenge needs to be presaged by the understanding that the process always outweighs the outcome. Parents can often be the unwitting triggers for stress – particularly when it involves placing unrealistic demands upon their children. The onus again lies upon the teacher to educate the parents and align them with the principle that, whatever the result, all we ask is for the students to give their best and learn from the experience.

It's also important that the students themselves are given the tools required to deal with stress – and this includes closing the gap between expectation and capability. Or, to look at it in more practical terms, if you have a big test on Tuesday, the most practical way to avoid stress is to ensure that you are as well prepared as possible.

2. **Depression.** Students have a tendency to self-diagnose as being 'depressed' when they're feeling sad and we need to provide them with a clear understanding of what sets sadness and depression apart. We will all experience bad things in life (bereavement, disappointment, rejection, you name it) and, when those bad things occur, it's perfectly natural for us to feel sad. Depression rears its ugly head when that sadness refuses to budge, becomes all-consuming or even becomes *the thing* in itself, even when the original trigger has faded from memory. When left unchecked, depression can be completely overpowering and, in some cases, very dangerous. Parents who aren't particularly enlightened in their understanding of mental health issues will often (in the most well-meaning way) attempt to adopt a pragmatic response, in the same way that you would if your car had a faulty carburettor. In these instances, they will often seek to rationalise the situation and play down the source of the depression, stress or anxiety. Often

though, this particular trigger can be relatively interchangeable and, even if removed or neutralised, the person struggling will simply find another stressor to attach their feelings to. The key in these situations is to provide empathy and support, rather than immediately looking for a faulty part to fix. The last thing someone suffering from depression wants to hear is the source of their feelings being downplayed or diminished; what they often require is empathy, support and understanding. As such, 'I understand how you must feel; it will get better and I'm here to help' is a far more useful response than 'What are you worrying about that for?'

3. **Anxiety.** As with stress, anxiety is (in some respects) a perfectly natural response to a pressurised situation. If you have an important test in the morning, it's only to be expected that you may feel a little 'anxious', just as you might ahead of a first day in a new job or on a first date. *Anxiety* is what happens when you add rocket boosters to that feeling of anxiousness and it becomes in turn controlling, overpowering and ultimately crippling. In many instances this level of anxiety can be easy to spot and can be manifested in the most obvious of ways (shortness of breath, shaking, etc). Be warned though: anxiety can be a master of disguise and many of the most profound symptoms can be internalised. That committed student for whom *good enough* is never sufficient could be riddled with anxiety while presenting a calm face to the world; likewise that lovely kid who always seems desperate to please may be smiling on the outside but experiencing constant torment on the inside. Anxiety is a sneaky customer and you have to look out for it, even in the least obvious places.

This is far from an exhaustive list and these descriptions are not intended to act as clinical definitions. Your role as a teacher neither qualifies nor requires you to make clinical diagnoses or interventions. Instead, your focus should be on watching, listening, supporting, liaising with colleagues and families and, where required, signposting the young people concerned to the most appropriate services. More importantly, it's essential that we educate, demystify and normalise the subject of mental health and help all members of our communities to recognise and respond to the tell-tale signs in ourselves and others.

You could write several volumes detailing each of the threats that are currently out there and highlighting the many warning signs that precede them. The problem is that the moment it was published, each edition would almost certainly be obsolete. The only thing we can do in the face of an ever-changing and ever more challenging world is to stay informed, stay vigilant and be ready to respond.

CHAPTER 10:

Making every child matter

The phrase 'every child matters' was used as the tagline for a 2003 government initiative aimed in part at ensuring that no child – whatever their circumstance – was *invisible* or left behind. Whether the initiative was a success is open to debate but the one place those three words should still ring loud and clear is inside *your* classroom. Within that 10ft x 20ft room, you have the power to ensure that every child feels supported and valued, is listened to and is encouraged to reach their potential – whatever obstacles they may face.

Your ability to meet the needs of your students may be limited by factors beyond your control – not least the support and provision available within your school – but your willingness to fight (if needs be) for your students is strictly within your control. As challenging as this may be, it's always worth returning to the mantra 'Would this be good enough for my child?' in order to focus on the task ahead.

When making sure that 'every child matters' we are handed a predetermined set of characteristics all intended to act as shorthand for advantage/ disadvantage. Special Educational Needs and Disabilities (SEND), Free School Meals (FSM), Pupil Premium (PP), Looked After Children (LAC), English as a Second Language (ESL), Black, Asian and Minority Ethnic (BAME) ... the list of 'key characteristics' is practically endless. On a macro level these headings are, of course, necessary indicators when analysing statistical data. However, on a micro level (i.e. in your classroom!), while providing a useful guide, there is a danger that these labels could lead you down the wrong path and, for many children, could be inaccurate and limiting. The trick, as ever, is to get to know each of your children as individuals, with any supposedly determining characteristics providing *potential* context rather than defining the individual concerned.

> ### *It's always worth returning to the mantra 'Would this be good enough for my child?'*

If you adopt this nuanced and personalised response within your classroom, you will quickly see a number of misconceptions kicked into the long grass. English may well present difficulties for many dyslexic learners, yet Agatha Christie, Hans Christian Andersen and W B Yeats all purportedly defied the limitations of this particular form of neurodiversity and went on to do pretty well for themselves. There may well be a dyslexic Yeats or Christie in your classroom if you're willing to cast away limiting preconceptions and adopt a growth mindset. Similarly, when carving out time for intervention lessons, the received wisdom in many schools is to remove SEND learners from modern foreign languages lessons. However, this received wisdom fails to take into account the growing body of evidence which suggests that children with autism can not only benefit from learning another language but may even excel, providing the provision is appropriate.

The focus needs to be on foregrounding the things that your students can do particularly well, while working collaboratively to mitigate for those areas that may be more challenging. Once you've removed your blinkers, your focus then needs to be to convince each student that their own particular characteristic is something that they will need to work with, rather than something that limits or defines them.

There's a growing (and extremely encouraging) trend within schools to celebrate role models who have conquered their own difficulties to achieve success within their chosen field. Richard Branson (dyslexia), will.i.am (ADHD) and Daniel Radcliffe (dyspraxia) are among a host of famous names who are happy to talk about their difficulties and how they overcome them, while the explosion of social media platforms such as TikTok does at least provide the students with direct access to an endless supply of potential role models within their own peer group.

Teachers are also just as likely to enlighten their students about the benefits that their condition *may* offer rather than simply fixating on any potentially inhibiting factors. For instance, tech companies in Silicon Valley are not only recognising the huge value that autistic employees can offer but are even modifying their recruitment processes in order to remove any potential barriers to hiring the best possible staff. Closer to home, GCHQ has confirmed that when recruiting the next generation of James Bonds and George Smileys, candidates with dyslexia and other neurodiverse conditions are seen as potential assets, with a particular aptitude towards codebreaking and other key skills. Information like this can provide an empowering counter-narrative if presented in the right context. It's important, however, that we don't use this information to patronise or dismiss the significance of any particular SEND issue; a condition such as dyslexia may present challenges but it can also have benefits too.

Data and labels alone can often construct a false narrative.

Ethnicity and language can also sometimes be presented as an immovable barrier to success – but we must not allow this flawed orthodoxy to go unchallenged. As an English teacher, I've lost count of the number of times where it's been suggested by (non-specialist) senior academic leaders that it might be worth withdrawing ESL/SEND candidates from English literature examinations on a wholesale basis. For some candidates this *might* be a pragmatic move but for many others (even those who may struggle with literacy and the mechanics of language) there may be a real flair for inference waiting to be unlocked – not to mention the joy that can be derived from exploring great literature!

Although labels provide a useful basis for statistical analysis, when you *zoom in* and focus on the kids who are actually sitting in front of you, they can often be misleading. Although Pupil A may tick many of the 'disadvantage' boxes, these characteristics may not always tell the real story. They may well return home to a council flat (✓) filled with books and spend a couple of precious hours discussing their schoolwork with their highly engaged and supportive single parent (✓). Meanwhile, affluent Pupil B might head to a big house up the road, retreat straight to their bedroom and spend the whole evening glued to their Xbox. In such a scenario, you have to ask yourself *which student is actually disadvantaged?*

When you are assigned a new class and furnished with both this information and a whole range of baseline data, it's important that this informs your planning and approach, but it's even more essential that you get to know each individual and trust your own judgement. Data and labels alone can often construct a false narrative.

Creating the culture and conditions for success

Once you have taken the time to get to know your classes and have been able to gauge how your own assessment measures up to the baseline data, it's time to start establishing a climate and culture where each student can achieve their full potential. When doing this, you need to focus on one word, as do your students: *ambition*. Whatever challenges you may be presented with and whatever support and intervention you may have to implement, ambition has to be at the centre of everything you do.

People often look at ambition in very narrow and distant terms. When talking to children, the topic of ambition is often framed around a question that for many children may still be intangible: 'What do you want to do when you grow up?' We need to strip that back and look at ambition and aspiration with a much more short-term focus – namely being willing to embrace challenge and striving for the best possible outcome from each task. It is also essential that *ambition* is divorced from *competition*. While friendly competition, based around carefully constructed groups, can make revision activities more engaging (it never ceases to amaze me how a PowerPoint version of the 1980s TV gameshow *Blockbusters* can make students so keen to revise key terms!), it's important that we reinforce the message that each student is only ever *competing* to be the best version of themselves.

Once you have established a culture where each student can achieve their potential, you need to focus on one word: ambition.

That culture of ambition has to radiate from you, however. When faced with difficult groups, it can often be tempting to lower the bar and pander to perceived limitations. In the same situations, teachers will sometimes look at their class list, examine the SEND codes by each student's name, and immediately start handing out differentiated worksheets and putting scaffolding in place. Not only is this disempowering but it can also fail to prepare the students for those occasions (e.g. public examinations) when that scaffolding is no longer available.

Children will respond to challenge when it's presented to them by someone who not only believes in them but also establishes a clear understanding that, if you aim for the highest bar, it's OK if you sometimes fall short, as long as you do your best. What's more, when framed correctly (and occasionally creatively), challenge can actually become a motivating badge of honour. Try telling your Year 8 class, 'My Year 10s couldn't manage this last year but I reckon you lot can smash it' and watch how keen they are to pick up that mantle. This might sound fanciful but try it; if you get the culture right, it really does work!

Of course, when all is said and done, not every student is going to meet the high bar you've set and some of them are going to need a ladder (or at least a leg-up) to get there. This is where your planning, your use of scaffolding and your understanding of each individual all become imperative. When you commit to introducing challenge, you'll know which of your students risk feeling immediately overwhelmed and may (initially at least) require additional support or differentiated tasks and materials. There will, however, be others who – although it might eventually be necessary to implement similar support – *may* be able to manage the work without intervention. It's important that you instil those children with the confidence to not only give it a go but also the security to request the additional scaffolding if it's all a bit too much.

At the other end of the scale, it's equally important to have a more challenging task up your sleeve that other more able students can attempt, while being equally secure in the understanding that failure is an intrinsic feature of learning. If you can factor different levels of differentiation into your planning and provide the students with an element of (guided) choice, it enables them to be ambitious and grow in confidence and aptitude. There's nothing more satisfying than witnessing a student who may previously have perceived themselves as *less able* ask you (invariably with a smile on their face), 'Can I have a go at the Challenge Task today?' That ambition has to start with you.

Once you have that culture embedded, it's important that you reward it as often and effectively as you can. The success of this again pivots around your understanding of each individual within the group. Your school will have its own rewards system and whatever you do will need to be framed around this. For some students, a moment of glory in the spotlight and praise in front of their classmates will be manna from heaven. For others, however, such undue public attention may be their worst nightmare, but a discreet word at the end of the lesson (or even a quick email to parents) will give them a timely (and often lasting) boost. Your judgement is essential but, whatever the appropriate response, your use of praise should never be taken for granted, has to be vocalised and needs to amount to more than simply popping a sticker in a planner. The only way to embed a positive culture is to consistently recognise and reward the behaviours that contribute to it.

If you can factor different levels of differentiation into your planning and provide the students with an element of guided choice, it enables them to be ambitious and grow in confidence and aptitude.

In doing this, it's also important that we continue to remind ourselves that success really does come in all shapes and sizes. Calvin's grade 9 essay and Carrie's grade 4 submission may look drastically different (on face value) but, when you factor in their differing starting points and the similar level of effort they required, the level of praise needs to be the same – even if the nature of delivery remains bespoke.

Once you factor in this approach, it really does become much easier to make *every child matter* – even when teaching mixed ability groups. As an English teacher, it is always my preference to remove the glass ceiling of setting until it becomes a practical necessity. In my subject at least, an inclusive classroom can actually be beneficial but, whatever the context, the principles remain the same: understand the individuals; instil ambition; remove the crippling fear of failure; recognise hard work; reward *success* (whatever form that takes) for each individual.

Making the most of your teaching assistant

When you have children with additional needs in your class, the presence of a teaching assistant (TA) can be an absolute game-changer. Having started my own career in education in this role, I can also bear witness to the fact that TAs are often utilised ineffectively and occasionally treated as little more than hired help. If you see your TA's role primarily as someone to hand out the books and 'keep Jordan quiet' you are failing to make adequate use of a vital asset who could have a huge impact on both your ability to teach and the overall attainment of your class.

TAs aren't there to plan and deliver lessons, they aren't there to mark books and they certainly aren't there to manage behaviour (all of those things come under your remit). But they can be a huge asset if given direction and trust and if you are able to develop a successful partnership.

The other misconception to dispel is that your TA isn't there to work exclusively with the SEND students. They may well be assigned to a particular individual but their presence is there to ensure that you can deliver the appropriate outcomes to the whole class. Sometimes that may involve you working one-to-one with the designated student, while your TA holds the fort elsewhere. Developing a trusting and equal partnership will furnish you with that flexibility.

Unfortunately, I have occasionally seen teachers practically abdicating responsibility for their SEND learners to their TAs. This, again, is totally inappropriate and means that the person who is most qualified to teach your students (i.e. you) will be spending the least amount of time with those individuals who need your input the most.

The best working relationships with TAs occur when there is a true sense of partnership and shared purpose and where the TA is given access to the planning and is also invited to reflect on the success of the lesson with you (this will help your teaching too – no matter how many miles you have on the clock yourself). If things are working as they should and the culture within your classroom is where it needs to be, your TA will be an intrinsic part of your class and will be free to move around the room, providing support without any fear of stigma for the recipient.

The very best TAs are basically teachers in waiting; all they might need to make that next step is support and encouragement. If you're blessed enough to be working alongside one of these hidden gems, use your platform to give them that friendly nudge in the right direction. Our *raison d'être* is to empower those around us and encourage them to fulfil their potential – and that includes our colleagues too.

Don't forget your other important 'partners'

While your TA may be a visible and valued presence within the classroom, it's easy to forget about one set of *colleagues* whose role is invaluable – particularly when working with SEND children. The importance of collaborative relationships with parents is writ large elsewhere in this book but, when working with SEND students (or indeed students with other potential barriers to learning), strong ties and regular communication are priceless.

This level of communication is particularly important when setting homework and can strengthen your ability to instil ambition and present challenge. It may be inappropriate to set work at a level that requires support from parents but, providing you have already invested in the relationship, it can be helpful to pre-warn parents if a particular assignment has the potential to be challenging and to provide them with alternative work if required.

If you can instil in parents the understanding that you are working in partnership and each want the best possible outcome for their child, then this kind of partnership can be transformative for students with additional needs.

Empathy is everything

The number of designated characteristics that can be assigned to the individuals within your class is seemingly endless, while there are likely to be others within your group who don't have a particular label attached but are just as needy – if not more so. Whatever the case, the most important skill you possess is empathy. Some people are born with empathy and can even carry the feelings of others so much that they can almost feel overpowering; some people find it a little more difficult to follow the advice of Atticus Finch and 'climb into someone else's skin and walk around in it.' Whatever the case, empathy is a skill and, if you're going to be a truly effective teacher, it's one you'll need to develop.

You may never have been diagnosed with dyslexia but it's important that you can consider how it must feel when the incredible ideas you might have in your head won't flow naturally onto a page. And you might have enjoyed a stable and privileged upbringing and may have loved school, but you need to find time to consider how different your experience may have been without that cosy upbringing, without the assumption of a hot meal at the end of each day and how different your relationship with teachers might have been had all the adults in your life let you down and failed to meet your basic needs.

Empathy is a skill and, if you're going to be a truly effective teacher, it's one you'll need to develop.

In order to have empathy you must first have understanding and unfortunately that can often require an investment of even more of your time. You could well be faced with a situation whereby a student seems to lie habitually and has even been caught stealing. Your natural inclination may well (justifiably) be to *throw the book at* that particular individual. Yet sometimes your natural inclinations need to be tempered by understanding and empathy.

What if that individual suffered neglect at an early age? And what if your subsequent research into attachment disorder led you to understand that lying is practically hardwired into those children who have been denied the barest necessities during infancy and, for those same children, stealing and hoarding are basic survival instincts rather than deadly sins? Armed with that knowledge and understanding, would your natural inclination be the same? Or would empathy guide you to a different response?

Whether operating within the confines of your own classroom or if you gravitate towards a leadership role later in your career, your ability to understand and empathise should guide everything you do.

Don't overlook your 'high flyers'

When considering how to make every child matter and taking into account the myriad of inhibitors that a child could be faced with, it would be impossible to even attempt an exhaustive list. You could work hard to ensure that the needs of your SEND students are met fully and that any stigma surrounding these issues is kicked firmly into touch. You might have armed yourself with knowledge and understanding of some of the cultural factors that may limit some of your other learners and have considered ways to mitigate these difficulties. And you may hopefully have explored the attainment gap between boys and girls and picked up a few nifty strategies to tackle this thorny issue. Whatever the circumstance or challenge you are faced with, your ability to really *see* each individual and gain an understanding of how best to meet their needs will be the thing that defines your success or failure. This will require you to bow to the expertise of colleagues (including your SENCO and your ESL Coordinator), do plenty of background reading and, above all else, invest the time required to get to know each individual.

All of this piles even more weight on your shoulders and will demand even more of your time and, in the midst of all this, you might just overlook one particular group: your potential *high flyers*.

We are often – rightly – told to beware of the 'invisible kids'. The received wisdom among teachers is that, among the bright sparks, the disruptive influences and the needy, there is another constituency of kids who aren't particularly academic, don't cause any bother and therefore get forgotten. Those children are definitely out there – we have a name for them after all – and we need to look out for them. But it's that other group who I'm really intrigued by: those kids who have a hitherto undiscovered gift (one that they're probably not even aware of themselves), a gift that's just waiting to be unearthed and polished and, given the right encouragement, could change the world. With all the other things you've got going on, it's not surprising that we might be overlooking these kids but I'm convinced they're out there. Let's find them!

CHAPTER 11:

Looking after yourself

I am conscious of the fact that the last 10 chapters all seem to hinge upon the common theme of you having to conjure up time and energy that doesn't actually exist. Unfortunately, that's one of the realities of the job; contrary to what you may have read in the right-wing press, nobody gets into teaching for an easy life. But if you're going to last the course and if you're going to be able to look after other people, you're going to have to learn how to look after yourself too.

I'm writing this at an age where, had I moved into teaching straight from university, I'd still only be halfway towards retiring on a full pension. Teaching has arguably never been more physically and emotionally demanding than it is right now, yet, if you're to cash in that mythical 'gold-plated pension' that the *Daily Mail* keeps telling its readers about, you face the prospect of keeping this up until you're 68. That's a scary thought!

For the sake of your own sanity, it's probably best to focus on the here and now and for many teachers that might simply amount to making it through to the end of the next week (or even day!). Sadly, there isn't a miracle cure to fix this and there definitely isn't a one-size-fits-all approach but the following ideas might just guide you towards a way forward that works for you.

Understand your mental health

Lots of schools seem to be getting on board with mental health (albeit in a fairly superficial manner) but we've clearly got a long way to go. It's OK for a member of SLT to stand in front of a PowerPoint presentation and spew platitudes like 'It's OK not to be OK' but, if the experience of you and your colleagues tells you that's not actually the case, these are nothing more than empty words. Similarly, staff yoga, knitting, table tennis, etc might look great on your school's Twitter feed but, if they are not backed up by regular substantive reviews of your working practices and access to meaningful support, then it's little more than window dressing (at best).

Thankfully, there are some schools that are pushing beyond the superficial and taking the duty of care for their staff seriously. I was really pleased to hear about a local school that recently gave all of its teaching staff a day off in order to focus on writing their reports, while there are a growing number of others who recognise that paying for professional counselling and support is an investment rather than a liability. There are still plenty more who have a lot of catching up to do though so, in the short term at least, we teachers owe a duty of care to ourselves.

I've written already about the importance of educating ourselves about mental health (and particularly the 'big three' of stress, depression and anxiety) but it's essential that we apply that self-care to ourselves. We need to understand these conditions and the impact they can have; we need to be able to spot the signs – in both ourselves and others – and we need to know how to respond. We also need to ensure that we develop strong support networks within our workplaces, where it really is 'good to talk'. And collectively we need to gently nudge our employers to the realisation that 'it's OK not to be OK' is a medical imperative and not just a soundbite.

Establish a 'work–life balance' that works for you

The phrase 'work–life balance' is one that's likely to invoke either a quizzical look or a hysterical guffaw when uttered in front of most teachers. Yes, we know that we have good holidays, but we don't half earn them and there are too many colleagues out there who wish the bulk of their lives away dreading the Sunday night fear or counting 'sleeps' until the next half-term break. That's no way to live, it's enough to prompt a growing number of colleagues to seek gainful employment elsewhere and, if you're going to last in this profession, you're going to have to re-evaluate your approach to work and life.

Part of the solution lies within establishing a pattern or structure that is sustainable and fits around the rest of your life. For some colleagues that involves utilising every spare second while they are at school (including break and lunch) in order to ensure that they are able to draw a very clear and divisible line between school and home. Other colleagues rely on the respite of a coffee in the staffroom during a frenetic working day so have to establish their own routines.

The one *thin red line* I'd always advocate is doing whatever you can to keep the threshold of your home sacred. The 2020 lockdown put a huge strain on teachers for all sorts of reasons but that erosion of the necessary boundaries between home and work was almost certainly at the heart of it. Like most teachers, I routinely have to bring marking etc home but my own golden rule is that those books never make their way from my car to the house and instead I endeavour to fit a set time slot around family life, where I do my marking in the corner of my local Costa Coffee (other coffee shops are available). This is a self-imposed rule that works for me; you need to find one that works for you.

Before you do that though, make sure you reflect back on the wise words of Derek, my old PGCE tutor: 'Never try to be *too good*.'

When the work you've done is good enough and it's time to stop, *stop*.

Prioritise 'me time'

This one needs carving in stone: you have to find time to do the things you enjoy and the things that make you *you*. With books to mark, lessons to plan and sheer, overwhelming tiredness to contend with, it's understandable that the first casualties of our careers in teaching tend to be the things that we love to do the most – and that's before you start throwing family commitments into the mix.

When keeping an eye out for depression and stress, losing enthusiasm for the things you enjoy can often be a key indicator. Yet, as teachers, we do this routinely. When figuring out a structure or routine that works for you, you really can't afford to neglect those activities that keep you healthy and sane. So, before you even consider when you're going to mark your books, first ensure that you've committed a time to horse riding, kickboxing or whichever other activity gives you a deserved break from being a teacher. And, once you've put that programme in place, stick to it, come hell or high water.

Have the right conversations with the right people

Yes, it is good to talk. And, yes, it is important that you don't bottle up your feelings and emotions. But it's also important that you choose the right people to talk to.

It goes without saying that your chosen confidantes need to be people you trust but they also need to be the kind of people that guide you towards a better place.

As the old adage goes 'misery loves company'. Joining the *negative corner* in the staffroom might be cathartic in the short term and it does you no harm to have a good moan from time to time but, if you linger too long, being part of that echo chamber of negativity will weigh you down and do nothing to elevate the way that you feel.

Try to choose a tribe that's trustworthy, supportive, funny, pragmatic but, ultimately, positive.

Opt for safety in numbers

This one boils down to a fairly simple and didactic message: join a union. It might seem like money for nothing and, if you're lucky, you might go your whole career without ever needing to call upon their support but when you do need them...

There's a tendency in one or two schools to try to banish unions from the premises and encourage the creation of 'Staff Consultation Committees' (or similarly labelled quangos) as a means of controlling any potential dissent. This strikes me as being akin to Kim Jong-un forming his own opposition party and then declaring North Korea a fully functioning democracy. I can see why some school leaders are fearful of a union presence within their schools and I am also aware of occasions when some unions have behaved in an unnecessarily obstructive manner but a strong staff voice is an essential organ within a healthy school and union affiliation is an important part of that.

Our unions do sometimes pick the wrong fights and can occasionally have a tendency to prioritise the political over the practical but they still play a vital role in providing teachers with a strong collective voice.

Confident leaders will welcome a strong staff voice and will understand that polite *conflict* usually heralds sensible resolutions. However, when faced with those who aren't as receptive to this form of engagement, it's essential that staff are able to stand shoulder to shoulder.

Be prepared to 'walk'

If you follow each of these steps and it still doesn't feel right, and if the Sunday night fear moves from being butterflies in your tummy to pounding in your chest, it's probably time to find another job. A former colleague of mine once compared being stuck in the wrong school to being trapped in a bad marriage and sensibly concluded that it was 'time for a divorce'.

It's also worth looking out for the writing on the wall even if you are at a school that you like. If you find your loyalty being taken for granted or even weaponised against you, it's probably time to be looking elsewhere because the one thing I can guarantee to you is this: no matter how invested you may feel in a place of work, that loyalty will not always be fully reciprocated.

You've chosen this career path precisely because you are committed, loyal and have a clear sense of purpose but, when your gut feeling tells you that it's time to go, walk.

If you do find that your career is having an adverse effect on your wellbeing, you may be tempted to think that the situation at your school is 'normal' or 'just the way things are' – particularly if you're new to the profession – but it isn't. Despite the lingering presence of a few bad eggs, there are plenty of outstanding leaders out there who run schools where the wellbeing of the students and the staff is paramount; make it your mission to find them and work for them. If you do, you'll never look back.

CHAPTER 12:
Integrity

Whenever you log onto social media and you see your friends from university 'living their best lives', venturing on expensive holidays and dwelling in a bigger house than you, you'll receive a timely reminder (if it was ever needed) that you didn't opt for a career in education for the financial rewards. The things that did lead you down this challenging path are likely to have been your values and your commitment to service to others. At the heart of both of these things is your integrity and, just as you entered the profession with these high ideals, you need to fight hard to leave it in the same way.

Unfortunately, at times in your career, your integrity may be challenged, both by the *carrot* and by the *stick*. Invariably, that carrot will manifest itself in the shape of your own ambition and you may be faced with a decision over what's most important to you: your values or the next big job. If you happen to land in the wrong school, you may find that you can't necessarily have both and your ability to nod, smile and look the other way will determine how far you are able to climb the ladder.

> *Just as you entered the profession with high ideals, you need to fight hard to leave it in the same way.*

In these particular organisations, once the older staff have been moved on, there's also a tendency to hook their replacements in with wild promises of a fast-track to SLT ('You could be a principal within five years'). For some young hopefuls these promises inevitably lead to disappointment, while for others there may well be the chance to leapfrog a few years in their development process (although at what cost?). Each of us needs to decide for ourselves what is more important to us: our ambition or our values.

For my part, I entered teaching at a relatively advanced age without any real preconceptions. Like my colleague Lesley (chapter 1), my initial ambition was simply to be an outstanding teacher. Over time that evolved partly due to the realisation that a) I could make more of a positive difference from a senior position and b) if I didn't make the move up the ladder, there was a very real prospect of spending the next 25-30 years having my career being dictated by other people. Ambition is a good thing; we should encourage it in our students and shouldn't hesitate to pursue it ourselves. We just need to be wary of blind ambition.

When looking up at the ladder, it's always important that you only go for roles where you are confident that you can add value and where the values of the organisation are closely aligned with your own.

Whichever route you do take, don't be tempted to abandon your principles along the way. Compromising on your principles can form a slippery slope; after you've done it once, it becomes easier to cross that line and, over time, the scale of those compromises can get bigger. And, if you're not careful, you'll soon reach a point where you're not the person you set out to be.

Over the course of your career, there's also a chance you may find yourself sitting in an assembly, listening to a senior colleague waxing lyrical about Rosa Parks or Martin Luther King or reciting the words of Peter Dale Wimbrow Sr as he/she urges the listener not to abandon their principles and end up cheating 'the man in the glass'. During these assemblies, several of your colleagues may well be unable to make eye contact and there'll be looks of incredulity from some of the kids too, because they'll know that this person does not practise what they preach. However far your career takes you, try not to be that person.

There's an abundance of amazing, principled and inspirational leaders doing incredible things in the world of teaching. There's even a whole community of them on social media who freely dispense support, advice and encouragement on a daily basis. Make it your business to find one of them, work for them, learn from them and – once the time is right – be like them.

Compromising on your principles can form a slippery slope; after you've done it once, it becomes easier to cross that line and, over time, the scale of those compromises can get bigger.

If and when you work your way into a position of influence, do it on your terms, with your values at the centre of everything you do and with your integrity intact. The journey might take longer, it might even be a little tougher but you'll be a better leader for it.

Once there, remember the Peter Parker principle ('with great power comes great responsibility'), never lose sight of the challenges you faced (and which your colleagues still face) as a humble classroom teacher and make sure you use your position of influence to make positive change. Effective policies are essential but your values, ethics and actions are even more important and the best policies are a manifestation of those three things.

For those of you at the start of your journey, try to figure out your own guiding principles. They may adapt over time but they shouldn't be sacrificed. For those of you who have already put in the hard yards, stick with it, stay patient and keep believing in yourself. We need more people like you in positions of influence. Getting there might be tough but we need *you*, not a cheapened (or compromised) facsimile.

After nearly two decades of working in education, my guiding principles have been pretty constant and, although I still harbour plenty of ambition, are likely to remain rooted around the same three questions:

1. Is the service I'm providing to these children and their families good enough?
2. Am I being true to myself and my values?
3. Would this be good enough for my own children?

You'll choose your own path and your own guiding principles but your integrity will have to lie at the core of both. Your integrity shouldn't be something that you're willing to sacrifice – even on the altar of your ambition – but it is something that can come with a cost attached. Sadly, there may be times when you encounter people whose values do not align with your own and, if you do come across these people, there's a chance that your own moral compass might position you squarely in their crosshairs. It's at these moments in your career that you need to consider what drew you to this job in the first place and what value you place on your own ethics.

Equally, there may be people who – for whatever reason – don't seem to like or rate you. As I made clear at the outset, it's at these times that you have to make a conscious decision about whose opinion you actually value or trust. More importantly, you need to ask yourself who your boss actually is. Is it the person with the big office and the reserved parking space? Is it the parent whose gratitude can barely be contained and can't be expressed in words alone? Or is it the child whose life is so much better because of the impact that you've had? Only the man in the glass can answer that.